Align + Attract

Align Your Energy to Create a Business you *Actually* Love

By Kerry Rowett

Cataloguing-in-Publication data is available from the National Library of Australia.

Rowett, Kerry
Align + Attract: Align Your Energy to Create a Business you *Actually* Love
ISBN 978-0-6483998-0-3 (print)
ISBN 978-0-6483998-1-0 (digital)

Editing: Natasha Gilmour - natashagilmour.com
Cover and web design: Dani Hunt - neverlandstudio.com.au
Cover photos: Emma Hannan - lifeslightcreative.com
Interior design: Ida Jansson - amygdaladesign.net

To my wonderful Mum, Roz, and sister, Anita, who are both so supportive and who have both always known I would write a book (at least one!).

To my loving partner Shaun who grounds me and our family. Thank you for always encouraging me to be the full version of me and believing in me and all I do. You are just so good for me. I love you.

To my sweet son Charlie, who we adore, and who is a total Mama's boy. You teach me that life is way more important than business, and that if you stay focused on your big picture, details and timelines fall into place when they're meant to. After nearly finishing this book before you arrived, it was well over a year before I returned to complete it, so immersed I was in our little world. The book is better for the integration time and I am better for all the time I am spending with you.

Thanks so much to my lovely friends Ezzie Spencer, Sara Brooke and Elena Pilch for your support and early feedback. And much gratitude to all the wonderful clients I have worked with since 2009, both one-on-one and in programs, and special thanks to those of you in my Align + Attract group program. You inspire me!

CONTENTS

INTRODUCTION

Would you love to create and grow an aligned business? A business that is heart-centred and reflects your values that you've consciously created to be sustainable and supportive of the way you want to live and work. The truth is, many of us start out in business feeling very inspired and aligned, but that initial excitement can soon give way to long hours, unexpected hurdles, fear, anxiety, doubt, confusion or overwhelm—or all of the above. You can start to wonder if you're on the right path after all. Things just might not be working. You can become trapped in a cycle of looking outside yourself for solutions, rather than nurturing your own ability to discern what is best for you and your business. Perhaps you join another course or sign up for another coach, hoping that this time, you'll find the missing link and create the success you crave, only to hit up against another dead end a little further down the road. Although, I wouldn't have articulated it that way back when I started my Kinesiology business in 2009, creating an aligned business was exactly what I set out to do. I was clear on the kinds of issues I was passionate about and could help others with. I focused on talking directly to my ideal clients, providing useful resources and sharing how I could help them. At that time, blogging was emerging, and I blogged regularly, posted a little on Facebook (at Awaken Kinesiology) and started a regular newsletter. And, because I am a Kinesiologist, I kept asking myself: 'What do I really want?' I used all my tools and spent a lot of time aligning my own energy to my goals, and releasing the fears, doubts and worries that came up as I embarked on my entrepreneurial journey. I went along to Kinesiology sessions regularly with a successful Kinesiologist (Amanda Adey) and aligned my own energy regularly to keep coming back to my own centre, so I could feel clear, focused and grounded and take actions that moved me closer to creating the kind of business I wanted. I began my business slowly, seeing my Kinesiology clients just one afternoon a week whilst still working nearly full-time in another job. The following year I focused on building my clientele to a full-time capacity, which I achieved. In 2011, I won a series of three business-coaching sessions (with then business coach Margaret Gill). How exciting! When she found out I was already booked out with clients she said right away, "You're obviously doing something right. You just need to find out what it is and bottle it." I knew the answer straight away: ALIGNMENT. Ever since starting my business, I consistently found and released any internal blocks I had to creating what I desired, and aligned my thoughts, words, actions and feelings with my intentions. I walked my talk. I stayed focused on my beautiful clients and how I could help them, and continued to attract more and more clients. After recognising that alignment had been THE key to my success, immediately, I began to download all I knew about alignment. First, a process arrived, which I called the Alignment Process. This channelled process was a streamlined version of the way I had cleared my own blocks and aligned my energy with my business goals. Despite my own trepidation about showing up and sharing this work, and with a big push from Marg, I first taught the process to other business owners in a simple program in 2011. I was thrilled to see it working so well for other practitioners. I expanded on that early work and have been teaching alignment ever since, most recently teaching coaches, healers, creative and heart-based business owners of all kinds how to clear their blocks and align their own energy to their business goals in my group program: *Align + Attract*.

The concepts you'll read about in this book underpin the program. I wrote this book to show how easy it is to fall out of alignment when we're in business, the questions we can ask ourselves, and the kinds of mindset shifts we can make to continue to come back into alignment. In this book you'll see (fictitious) Anna hit up against the kinds of challenges we all face, and progressively come into a greater state of alignment. Like many of us who embark on the path to creating a heart-based business, Anna is smart and capable, but also gets in her own way. She has to continue to problem-solve and shift back into a resourceful space so she can make choices, take action, and grow her business. You might find yourself relating to some of the questions she asks, issues she works through, and decisions she grapples with. Anna is a composite of the hundreds of entrepreneurial clients I've worked with since starting my Kinesiology business and in my *Align + Attract* program. She and I share some traits; maybe you do too. She's got some great qualities but she's not at all perfect, she experiences doubt, she obsesses, she judges at times, she feels envy. She's just a regular person. Anna is on the same journey you are on. She is trying to figure out what she wants and works towards creating it, course correcting where necessary. Your life and business choices will be different to hers. She's not a model for you to follow; she's a companion for you to walk with. If you find yourself thinking things like, 'That won't work! I'd do this instead', or otherwise disagreeing with Anna, that's good news. The process is working. You are further activating your own personal power and ability to discern what's right for you. Along with being the story of Anna's journey towards greater alignment, this book is also part guidebook. I recommend that you read the book slowly, taking time to answer the questions I pose in your free downloadable journal that is a companion to the book: alignandattract.com/journal. If you just race through this book, you're likely to become overwhelmed. You'll probably end up with a headache. You'll have many realisations and ideas sparked, but if you don't channel these somewhere, alignment will continue to be a nice theory or buzz word, rather than something you're actively creating in your own business. Take your time. Allow yourself time and space to reflect and integrate. My intention is not just to entertain you via Anna's story. My intention is that you'll use the sparks ignited as you read her story to create your own transformation. In this book, we focus on questions you can ask yourself and what you can do to create more alignment yourself. You need to do your own reflection, exactly as Anna does throughout this book. There are no short cuts or magic bullets that are guaranteed to help you create the business you want. That magical system, funnel, or social media hack that's working today, probably won't work in another few months or a year. Equally, an excessive focus on *manifesting*, being positive or visualizing what you want without consistent action is unlikely to reap the results you crave. Take the time to ask yourself what YOU want and experiment to find out what works in your business, and to attract the clients or customers YOU desire through the hard work of trial and error and taking action in the real world. Specific tools change fast and you're not going to learn HOW to attract more clients in this book. The approaches that Anna experiments with will date. You will have your own strengths and preferences and there will always be new tools and trends. What you will learn in this book is how to continue to come back to your own centre and discern what is best for YOU and what works in YOUR business. That's how you create a business you actually love.

Set your own intention now to create more alignment in your business and commit to doing your own reflections so you can kick-start the change and growth you crave. Alignment is powerful, but it doesn't guarantee outcomes. It doesn't mean you'll make $x a month or get y number of sign ups to your course. You can't use alignment as a tool to control and manipulate your life. However, being in alignment can certainly mean you're in the right place to take the actions that lead to the kinds of results you desire, and to respond appropriately when things aren't working the way you hoped. Alignment is certainly a process, not a destination. Just when you're feeling perfectly aligned, something new will pop up. After struggling to attract enough clients, you might find yourself fully booked, and need to create new boundaries, or increase your rates. Just as your business model seems to be working beautifully, you might expand your family or move locations and need to make changes. From a place of alignment, you can also let go of things that aren't serving you, or pivot direction. As you grow and evolve, what you want will change, and you will respond to this and allow yourself to continue to make new choices. Of course, there's work involved in creating and growing a business, but when you're aligned, you take action from a place of ease and flow rather than struggle and challenge. You consider your whole self and your whole life. You put yourself before your business. So, before you start reading Anna's story, download and print your copy of the journal: alignandattract.com/journal.

Are you ready? Let's start getting aligned.
Much love, *Kerry* xx

alignandattract.com
awakenkinesiology.com

Join me on Facebook: **/awakenkinesiology** and Instagram: **/kerryrowett**
Share your reflections as you read using the hashtag: **#alignandattract**

GET HONEST
WITH YOURSELF

'I'm 100% aligned to being honest with myself.'

Anna's soy latte arrives and she absentmindedly takes a sip. She's scrolling through Instagram. There's Sally. She's in Paris, sipping champagne and her lifestyle business is blowing up. 'Sign up for a discovery call and this life could be yours, you too can have an effortless feminine business and make six figures,' she reads. *I thought Sally said a few months ago she was deep in debt and had no clients. That's weird,* thinks Anna. She keeps on scrolling. There's a selfie of Jessica with her green smoothie. She's fresh out of yoga and off to meditate in a park with her journal before a day of amazing health coaching clients. Anna can't remember the last time she meditated, went to a yoga class or drank a green smoothie. *Oops.* She doesn't know Jessica, so she doesn't realise Jessica is barely keeping her head above water as she continues to work full-time as she tries to build up her client base in the evenings and on weekends. Anna keeps scrolling. There's Geneva talking about her latest cleanse and how amazing she's feeling. 'How are you doing it?' someone comments. 'I'll PM you!' Geneva has replied. A few posts down someone else has written a similar post, but this time about the incredible vitamins they're taking. It's probably the same multi-level marketing company. Anna makes an audible sigh. She flicks across to her Facebook page. She sees her latest post got one like. From her Mum. *Seriously,* she thinks. *I'm sure it's not supposed to be this hard.* Just as she starts to think about the clients she has booked in for the coming week and stress about where on earth she's going to find more new clients, Alexa arrives.

"Oh, my God, I'm sorry I'm late, traffic!" she says as she hugs Anna hello.

"Totally fine, I've been working," Anna tells her.

"Oh, good! Is business going well? Are you loving it?"

Anna is about to tell her that of course it's going well. That she loves being a coach and it's amazing to help others change their lives. That it's awesome being able meet a friend in a cafe mid-morning. All those things are true. But when she opens her mouth, she ends up telling the whole truth. That she loves her clients, but she has nowhere near enough of them. That whenever she looks at her bank account she feels anxious and that she regularly calculates how long that money can last before she literally has to get a job. That she's started having uncomfortable discussions with her husband about when this business is going to take off, and how her family think she's weird for taking this path and still don't understand why she left her safe accounting career. That she hates it when friends ask how business is going. That it's embarrassing and awkward trying to come up with an honest but upbeat response when she really just feels like a failure. That she doesn't want to have to answer the question: 'Why don't you just get a job?' That yeah, it's great to be in a cafe now, but she'll be on her laptop til at least nine tonight because she feels really guilty when she's not working, especially when she's not making enough money. That she can't figure out whether she should sign up to learn about webinars, e-courses, sales funnels, money blocks or launch strategy next, even though she can't really afford any of these things and she hasn't finished the last three courses she signed up for. Anna admits that she has no idea how to get herself out there, plus she hates the idea of selling herself anyway. Everyone she follows online does the same kind of work she does and talks about the same kinds of things. She's pretty sure the market is oversaturated, not to mention the fact it's all been done before and done better too. That she doesn't know how to grow her reach online or get people to sign up. To anything. And that social media changes so rapidly and organic reach will be at zero sometime soon, so what's the point anyway. She admits she finds herself looking at those glamorous and seductive Facebook ads where people talk about making tens of thousands of dollars in just a few months even though they were struggling before they learnt the system they want to teach you; a modern-day rags-to-riches tale. She wonders if she should pay thousands to learn how to do that herself, even though she's 99% sure the system they use to do that is unsustainable at best or an unscrupulous pyramid scheme at worst. That everyone else seems to have the secret and knows how to attract lots of clients and make great money. That she feels like she's either floundering around making it up as she goes along, or trying to follow someone else's step-by-step system which feels kind of gross, and never quite works for her anyway. That's she's lost all her confidence and has started doubting if she's good at what she does. She worries about whether her clients are happy enough with their results. She gives 110% to every session, and often goes overtime or discounts her rates, just in case, even though she resents it later and suspects her fees are too low to start with. That she's not feeling healthy because she's started skipping meals, comfort eating and forgetting to exercise. She admits that when she has a busy day she sometimes feels drained and then worries what would happen if she did end up booked out. And that she wonders if she's even cut out for this. Maybe she's not meant to be in business. Maybe she's just not good enough.

"Oh, my God. Thank you for saying it," says Alexa. "I've been feeling the exact same way about my Kinesiology business. What are you going to do?"

"I have no idea, but I can't carry on this way. Yes, I want to do what I love. I want to make a difference. I want to feel like I'm living my purpose. But I don't want it to be like THIS."

ALIGN + ATTRACT REFLECTION

Okay, get out your journal now! (You already printed your copy, right? Find it at alignandattract.com/journal.) How much time are you spending scrolling, researching, thinking or reading about what others are doing at the moment? How is this impacting on you? How do you really feel about where you're at in your business? What's definitely NOT working for you in your business right now? Let it all out, you're about to start making changes and it's incredibly useful to recognise where you're at now.

FOCUS ON WHAT YOU DO WANT

'I am 100% aligned to focusing on what I want.'

Anna was surprised to find she felt a little better after admitting to Alexa exactly how she felt about her business. Sure, nothing had actually changed, but there was a sense of relief in being honest and declaring that things couldn't continue as they were. She sat absentmindedly leafing through the latest copy of a magazine she loved which often shared stories of creative and inspiring businesses, hoping the success of the entrepreneurs she was reading about would start to rub off onto her. She read about new start-ups experiencing huge growth. *I'd be terrified of making a wrong decision, or burning out,* she thought. She read about businesses that had navigated legal issues, or conflicts of different kinds. *This is why it's better being small. No one knows who I am. So much safer.* She read about influencers with huge social media numbers and lots of publicity. *I'd hate to be so visible. Imagine all the judgment and criticism that would come with that,* she shuddered. As she continued to scan the stories, the words, 'What do you want?' leapt off the page. Anna felt her mind go blank. What did she want? Well, she knew what she didn't want: what she had now. She knew she didn't want any of the downsides of success. She didn't want too much pain, or challenge, and certainly no criticism. What DID she want? How had she missed that kind of obvious, vital question? Anna felt herself shrink back into the chair as she realised she had never actually asked herself what she really wanted from her business. Sure, she had paid to get a logo, got some help to set up a website and had chosen a business name. She knew she wanted to attract clients and help them. In fact, that had become the main focus of her entire business, almost to the point of obsession. But what did she truly want? Maybe it was time to start thinking about that.

ALIGN + ATTRACT REFLECTION

Over to you! Get out your journal and answer the following questions: Where are you are focusing on what you don't want in your business? We'll dig into this question more deeply throughout the book, but what comes up when you ask yourself now: What do I want from my business?

BE TRUE TO YOU

'I am 100% aligned to being true to myself.'

As Anna began to think about what she wanted in her business, she was surprised to discover she had no idea. She found herself scrolling on Instagram. She saw highly stylized images with designer clothing and perfect hair and make-up in locations like Paris and New York. She didn't dress like that normally, and she'd only been to Paris once, but did she need to book a more glamorous photo shoot? Was that the problem. She saw people calling their followers' babe, gorgeous or beautiful. She didn't talk like that normally herself, but would that help her create more connection with potential clients? She saw people sharing pictures of artfully presented acai bowls, green smoothies, and turmeric lattes and super food salads. She didn't really work on health-related goals with her clients, but should she start sharing more pictures depicting the latest trends in health, so she seemed in touch. She saw people sharing photos working on their laptop in Bali, Hawaii or New Mexico, running events around the country, attending big conferences, participating in retreats connected to their latest mastermind, and taking photos with their business besties around the world. Did she need to travel more and create more connections internationally that might help her grow her business? Was that the missing link. She saw people sharing transparently about their day-to-day challenges with their relationship, family, money, business or health, taking make-up free selfies and expressing raw emotions. Was that it, did she need to be more "real" and "authentic" in this kind of way to connect with more people? Anna realised she was so caught up in other people's dreams and desires and their approaches to business, that she had completely lost connection to her own. She constantly doubted whether she was doing or saying the right things in the right way. And she was always looking at what other people were doing and getting inspiration from that rather than focusing on doing things in her own way and allowing her own personality to shine through online. Everyone said, 'be yourself,' but some days Anna felt like she didn't actually know who she was anyway, and especially not right now, so getting clear on how she wanted to show up in her business felt impossible.

In her old job, everything was defined. The pay. The dress code. The kind of work she did and where she did it. When she could take time off and what for. The kinds of clients she worked with. Other people decided all those things and she just went along with it, like everyone else in the company did. It hit her, even though she had taken the step to work for herself, she was still doing the same thing. She was still letting everyone else decide what her business might look like, what her dreams might be and how she might achieve them. Sure, it looked like she was making the decisions. But she was making them with the underlying assumption that there was a right way—and, that other people knew that right way—Anna cringed as it dawned on her what had been happening. Rather than her boss or an organization, it was now her peers who led the way. She watched what they did on social media and did pretty much the same thing. She read the articles, listened to the podcasts and watched the videos and webinars and followed the advice or got "inspiration" to share with her own audience. She did the courses that other people told her would lead to success and tried to follow the systems that seemed to be working for other people. If the systems didn't work for her, she decided that clearly there was something wrong with her. Suddenly it hit her, she was not going to learn more about what she did want by constantly focusing on what everyone else was doing. She had to stop giving her power away to other people and being so influenced by her peers. She had to start focusing on what she did want. She had to get clear on what was right for her and give herself permission to show up as herself. She needed to find her own way of connecting and sharing. There was nothing necessarily wrong with any of the approaches she was seeing online, but it didn't seem wise to cherry pick style, tone, topics or approaches from her favourite accounts. She'd just sound like a mishmash of all that was currently popular at best and inauthentic and unoriginal at worst. She needed to stop admiring AND judging what others were doing, and focus on herself, her brand and her own message. Rather than looking at what was on trend, what she thought she should be doing or trying to dissect what seemed to be working for others, she had to start being true to herself, and showing up and connecting in ways that were authentic to her.

ALIGN + ATTRACT REFLECTION

Time to get out your journal and reflect. What trends are you noticing online at the moment? Are YOU getting caught up in either admiring or judging what others are doing, or getting heavily influenced by whatever is currently popular in your corner of the online or business world? How is this playing out right now? Are you clear on your own message? Does anything need to change?

GET CLEAR ON WHAT YOU DO WANT

*'I am 100% aligned to being clear
on what I want.'*

Anna made herself a strong coffee. She got out her journal. She wrote one question at the top of the page: 'What do I want?' And she began to write: 'I want to create a successful business. For me, success is about doing what I love. It's about having choices. It's about working with people who are ready for change and who really enjoy and value our work together. It's about making great money. I want to feel secure and stable. I want to have a positive impact on the lives of others. I want to feel creative and inspired. I want a fun and full life outside of my work. I want to explore who I am and express from the heart. I want to feel clear on my own message. I want to feel my business is always growing and evolving and that the next steps unfold with ease. I want to live and work in ways that feel sustainable and expansive. I want to make a big impact in the world and get involved in issues and community projects. I want to write and have my work read by thousands of people.'

The last few statements made Anna wince a little. *Is that my ego?* she questioned herself. *Aren't those goals kind of ridiculous when I look at where I am now? Can I really declare I want such big things? Who cares?* she decided. *These are my dreams. I have to stop judging myself. It's fine if some of my goals seem unrealistic now and take a few years to bring to fruition; maybe I'll be ready for them by then. Maybe it's okay for me not to rush. It's going to take some time to bring this vision to life, so maybe it's okay that I flow with the opportunities that are around me.* And she realised, *Maybe I do have time to exercise and eat well, if I can actually grow this business in my own time frame and forget about what everyone else is doing.* Anna knew she still had a long way to go to get clear on how she wanted to show up in her business, but she was feeling more inspired than she had in ages. It was refreshing to simply focus on what she wanted. Of course, this would evolve and change and there was so much more to explore and develop, but she'd made a start. She felt like she was focusing on the right thing for now—what she *did* want. She had a feeling that the clearer she got around what she really wanted, the easier it was going to be to make other decisions moving forwards.

She picked up her phone and rang Alexa.

Everything she'd been thinking and writing about poured out, "I can't believe I was getting so caught up in what other people are doing rather than spending time getting really clear about what's important to me and what kind of business I really want."

Alexa got excited too, "Oooh, this is juicy!" she declared. "I have to go. I need to go figure out what I want too."

As Anna hung up, she knew something was shifting. She got back to her brainstorming.

ALIGN + ATTRACT REFLECTION

Okay, your turn! Open up your journal and start reflecting. You can go into as little or as much detail as you wish, but don't skip over this step. Reading about Anna's experience will be sparking some of your own ideas and you'll want to capture these while they're fresh and a little raw. Remember you're just writing for you, so don't self-edit or worry about what you should be wanting; that defeats the purpose! This is your chance to connect to your own desires, and these of course change over time. Think of the big picture rather than details.

Get started now. What do YOU want?

JOIN FORCES WITH YOUR BUSINESS

'I am aligned with my business.'

Alexa and Anna were back in a local cafe.

"I did exactly as you suggested," started Alexa. "And it was amazing! It was so nice to think about what's important to me rather than what I think I should want, or what I think is possible."

"Can you believe we'd never thought to do it before? How was that ever going to work out?!" Anna laughed.

"I know, right? Anyway. As soon as I finished, it occurred to me—maybe the business also has an energy of its own—I mean, I've heard people talk about that, but I had no idea what they really meant. But I had the idea to write a letter to my business to ask *it* what *it* wanted, and then to write a reply, and see what came up."

Anna's eyes were wide as she listened to Alexa summarise

the response her business had given her: 'There is no need for you to struggle so much. Things can be so much easier. Let go of needing to know how and keep taking your next steps forwards. Focus on your clients. Focus on what you really want. Play. Have fun. Experiment. Allow yourself to dream but stay focused on action too. Walk your talk and keep clearing your own blocks. Get creative and enjoy this phase of growth on ALL levels.'

As they carried on sharing and reflecting, Anna realised a sense of anticipation was starting to build in place of the low level anxiety and fear she usually felt when thinking about her business. Nothing had changed, yet, but she was starting to get a sense of why that might have been. She was feeling more optimistic and energised than she had in a while. Alexa headed off; she had clients booked and wanted to get organised. Anna had just two clients that day, one mid-afternoon, and one at 9 pm. She'd find it hard to sleep after the late session, but that time suited the client, so she accommodated. Usually she'd spend this expanse of time worrying and stressing and trying to connect in various Facebook groups, but today, she couldn't wait to connect with her business. She got out a piece of paper and began to write: 'Dear business, What do you want? What would make you happy, shining and sparkly? Love and hugs, Anna. xx'

Without thinking about it too much, she started to write her answer: 'Dear Anna, I want you to stop worrying about me. Your worry is stopping me from growing. It's keeping away your people. I want you to appreciate me. I grew enough that I allowed you to leave a job you described as Soul sucking, do I get thanks? No. Just more, more, more. Get me more clients and make me more money when all I am doing is supporting and protecting you because I love you. You need to treat me like the beautiful and sometimes still fragile gift that I am. I grow through love and care and watering. When you complain or worry about me I wonder what I can do that will ever make you happy and satisfied. Do you want me or do you just want more? Bless me, love me and tell me how wonderful I am. You nourish me with your words. Your words make me feel strong. When you write, I know that you understand me and what I'm here for. Your words connect you back to me. My wish is to be magnificent. I am beautiful. I am confident. I am becoming more visible. Enjoy me and have fun with me. I'm going to be around for a while and I want to grow. Love, your business. xx'

Anna sat back and re-read what she'd written. She didn't know whether to feel horrified, or to laugh at the accuracy of what had just come through. She wasn't completely sure where the answer had come from. Was it her higher self? Her guides? She didn't really know what people meant when they talked about these things, but she did know that the response she'd written felt useful, and it felt true. It had given her some ideas about where she was going wrong and what she did need to do.

ALIGN + ATTRACT REFLECTION

Your turn! Get out your journal (alignandattract.com/journal) and start your own letter. What does YOUR business want? Get started now. You can choose your own wording, or start your letter like this: 'Dear business, What do you want? What messages do you have for me? Love, me. xx' And then get started with your reply. Don't think too much about it, just write down whatever comes.

CONNECT FROM YOUR HEART

'I am 100% aligned to connecting from my heart.'

Anna was reflecting on her letter. She had to acknowledge that she had achieved some success in her business. She did have paying clients. Sure, there weren't quite enough to make things comfortable, and sure her business hadn't yet grown like she thought it would now that she was devoting all day every day to it, but there were certainly some positive signs. Anna thought about a couple of clients she had spoken to recently who felt really stuck. They were both starting to make some changes that were truly shifting things for them and it was so inspiring to see. What kind of message did she want to give to them? She opened her Facebook page and started to write: 'Do you ever look around at other people and feel envious that they seem to know exactly what to do, and exactly where they're going? I remember when I worked full-time as an accountant, I could see that some people loved that world. They loved climbing the ladder of success, the structure, the formality, the salary and perks. I used to feel envious of those who had found what they really wanted. It was the same when I first came across my coach—she helped me so much and seemed so excited about what she was doing—I felt envious that she had been able to change careers and do what she loved. And now I find that I'm here too. I've got a long way to go in creating the business I truly want and helping the numbers of people I'd love to help, but right now I'm thinking about a gorgeous client I've got coming up this afternoon, and another later today. A lot of my clients at the moment are learning to re-connect to joy, to finding their pleasure, to celebrating and feeling grateful. I am learning these lessons too, on an even deeper level than before. And right now, I am feeling so grateful for where I am, and where I'm heading. And I'm realising it's so important to celebrate our little successes. What are you grateful for right now?' Anna took a quick selfie of her smiling face in the cafe and hit publish on the post. *Oh, my God, that was easy,* she laughed. *Where did that come from?* It was a simple post, but it was truly from her heart, and in the moment, as compared to the "inspirational" quotes she usually shared, or the posts that she wrote and re-wrote and agonised over. She clicked on edit and added, 'If you'd love to feel more joy in each day and find your own pleasure, I work on this kind of thing with clients all the time. I'd love to help you too!' She inserted a link to her bookings page. As she clicked save, she noticed the post had two likes, and a comment from someone she didn't know, saying, 'This is so inspiring. I think I'm where you used to be right now!' As she replied, Anna was beaming. *Hmm, maybe I could write a blog post or do a Live and expand on these ideas,* she thought.

ALIGN + ATTRACT REFLECTION

Your turn: How do you feel about what you're sharing on social media? Do you feel like you're sharing and connecting in genuine and authentic ways? Are you inspired to share anything right now?

TAKE CONTROL

*'I am aligned with creating a great life
as well as a great business.'*

It was after ten at night. Anna had just finished with her client
and she sat mindlessly scrolling through Instagram on her
phone. Her husband sat next to her on the couch. She felt mildly
envious of the shiny, smiling images at Jane's latest goddess circle
and adoring comments below the image, and then noticed Sian's
followers had climbed past 10000.

"I'm so far behind," she sighed.

Next, reading an inspiring self-help quote from Lisa, 'Good
things come to those who hustle,' and the chimes of agreement
that followed, she was half-aware her husband was trying to get
her attention.

"Sorry, what was that?" she looked up, trying to hide her
mild annoyance.

"I was just asking if you wanted a cup of tea. You know, it's really hard to get your attention when you're playing on your phone like that. Can't you put it away at this time of night?"

Anna felt her frustration rise, "I am not playing on my phone. I am working. And I'm trying to wind down. It's been a long day. And yes please, I would like a cup of tea. And sorry."

Anna was aware her reply was taking on a slightly hysterical tone, quite out of proportion to the request. The truth was she really did find it hard to wind down when she worked late at night, which was quite often. She figured she had to. Her online calendar showed availability from 6 am to 9 pm. She didn't want anyone to miss out. They might book in with someone else instead. She very often spent her evenings on her phone in an attempt to relax. Even though she felt she was doing "research" or "getting inspiration" or "being engaged" she more often found herself comparing herself unfavourably to others, feeling disappointed in her progress, and even more convinced she had nothing important to share or say. She got up off the couch and took her phone upstairs, plugged it in and returned to her husband.

As he handed her a tea, she said, "You're right. I'm going to try and switch off more in the evenings. It's just such a habit, and it makes me feel like I'm doing something productive. I feel stressed that I'm not making more money. Everyone's always talking about hustling and I never feel like I'm doing enough. I should be doing more. You know, work a few years how most people won't so you can live like most people wish they could. How does that quote go?" she trailed off.

"I know the one," Josh laughed.

"I guess that would probably be more relevant if I was creating a multi-million-dollar start-up," Anna acknowledged. "Maybe it would be worth working all the time if I was going to sell the business and make millions in a few years, but that's not exactly what I'm working towards anyway."

Josh was nodding. "I know how passionate you are, babe. But I'm watching you working all these hours, stressing out, and not sleeping properly. You're not yourself. It's affecting us. Surely there's a different way?"

As they continued to talk, Anna felt relieved to be back working like a team again. She had the uncomfortable realisation that she'd been letting the business create a wedge between the two of them. She had been assuming that things would get better if she worked harder and had more money coming in. In fact, she had become fixated on this solution, working harder and harder and longer and longer hours, without stopping to pay attention to whether what she was doing was actually creating the results she desired. She thought that if she worked harder that would mean she'd end up making more money and that would solve all her problems. But was that really true? So far, in pursuit of her goal, all these long hours just seemed to be creating more issues. Now she had to deal with broken sleep, distance in her relationship, extra weight, a stiff and sore body from not enough exercise, sluggishness, anxiety, and a horrible wired anxious feeling that was starting to follow her everywhere she went. She was compulsively checking stats, page views, likes, her bank balance, and whether anyone had commented on her posts. When she wasn't "working" she was obsessing about something business related, and she felt guilty whenever she took time out. Anna had always worked hard and saw herself as successful but her high expectations and perfectionism were starting to work against her now that there were so many uncertainties, new things to learn, ways to quantify success and opportunities to compare herself to others. Instead of creating success, she seemed to be getting stuck in her head, overthinking everything, judging and criticizing herself and becoming exhausted. This wasn't why she'd started her own business. Anna knew something needed to change. Josh was very supportive, but she realised if she wanted to continue having a great relationship, she had to invest time and energy into it. It wasn't fair that she was constantly distracted and focused on the business all day and every night, and it clearly wasn't good for her health either. As her letter from her business had already told her, the worry had to stop. The obsessing had to stop. She opened up with Josh about how she was feeling about the business and why she felt like she had to focus on it so intensely. She was realising it was really a way of managing her anxiety and fear. She hated the idea of failure. It was easier to fixate on working harder than to face that fear, and to honestly acknowledge that she was still learning, and didn't really know what was going to happen in the business moving forwards.

"You aren't your business you know," Josh reminded her. "And your business isn't set in stone. It will change a lot over the next few years, and you'll get clearer on what you want."

"That's true," Anna agreed. "The business I end up running might end up being totally different to what I'm doing right now. I have to remember I'm still testing this business model. If something isn't working, I need to remember that it doesn't mean I am a failure. It just means I need to look at it and make changes. I've been taking it all way too personally, like I AM my business. But as you just said, I'm not. My letter from my business said that too. And then I already forgot." She laughed and shook her head.

As they talked, she came up with the beginnings of a plan. She decided she'd put her phone away after dinner to give her and Josh time to connect at night. She'd plug it in away from her bed, so she wasn't tempted to start scrolling when she woke up in the middle of the night. She knew that wasn't exactly helping her sleep. She was going to stop spending so much time on social media. She needed to tune into her own voice, her own thoughts, and share those. No more mindless scrolling. And it was time to do something about this perfectionism. She was done with it. And all the anxiety, worry and fear too. As she collapsed into bed that night, Anna felt a new feeling of control starting to emerge. *This is my business. I can run it in ways that suit me.*

ALIGN + ATTRACT REFLECTION

Your turn! Any reminders you need to give yourself about things you want to start doing or stop doing? Now is the time to get out your journal (alignandattract.com/journal) and write them down, while they're fresh. Use Anna's conversation and thoughts as a prompt, but then go deeper as you think about your own patterns and how they might be holding you back right now.

RELEASE WORRY
AND FEAR

'I am aligned to feeling relaxed and clear.'

Anna was reflecting on the letter she had written her business and one of the messages that had come through: 'I want you to stop worrying about me. Your worry is stopping me from growing.' It was true, and Anna knew it. She was constantly worrying about her business and every little thing that could go wrong. She already knew this had been a big driver behind her drive to work all the time. She knew that when she had time and space, the worries and fears came straight up to the surface. Working kept them suppressed. She'd touched on some of her fears in her conversation with Alexa at the cafe, and it was good to acknowledge how she really felt, but she hadn't addressed those fears yet. The truth was, now she was working for herself there seemed to be so many unknowns, and so many things outside of her control. She didn't know when her next client would book in. She couldn't be sure how much money she'd make each week. She didn't really know how long it would take to build momentum. The next steps weren't always clear; in fact, they usually weren't. Anna was often worrying about money, and whether she was making the right decisions, and sometimes got caught up obsessing about different negative scenarios. So much of the messaging that surrounded Anna told her that living in a state of fear was a pretty normal thing when you were in business. Some of the people she followed talked about the need to crush your fears, to take big risks, to invest big and reap the rewards from that. 'Feel the fear and do it anyway!' 'Push through!' 'Leap and the net will appear!' Those were the kinds of messages Anna was tuned into anyway. Well, she sure felt plenty of fear, but she had no idea whether it was helpful or constructive. It was hard to tell whether her fears were leading her closer to her dreams, or just down a pathway to stress and burnout. Truthfully, half the time Anna couldn't tell which fears were silly and just her mind running out of control, and which fears were actually her intuition telling her something was wrong. Anna found herself worrying and feeling bad she wasn't more fearless. She was pretty certain you had to be fearless to be a good entrepreneur. Maybe she just didn't have what it takes, she'd think. And then she'd worry some more; about the damage her worry was causing, and what she was manifesting with her worry. Wasn't she supposed to be positive all the time to create the life she wanted? Some of the self-help messages she read seemed to suggest that she should, so she had been trying as hard as she could to "be positive" even though a lot of the time that felt pretty fake, not to mention unhelpful. Trying to ignore or suppress the fears wasn't working. She felt stuck. She carried on working, her worries still at the back of her mind. The temptation to spend her time scrolling on social media or getting caught up in discussions in business groups to distract herself was strong, but she instead decided to start planning a webinar that would help her clients. *Maybe I could focus it on releasing worries,* she thought, which made her giggle. *That will help me focus on finding solutions that work for me when I'm feeling super worried, like now, and I bet others will find it useful too.* She started to think about approaches that had worked for her in the past, and what she might try now to release her worries. She opened a meditation app on her phone. *This is one thing that I know works. I have to remember to do it.* She found a short guided meditation and sat and breathed through it. Her shoulders dropped and the anxious feeling in her chest dissipated. What else could she try? Anna had heard about a technique called EFT and had watched a number of different videos on YouTube to figure out how it worked. She decided to start a long list of every fear she currently had. All of them. It started: * I'm scared I'm not good enough. * I'm worried I don't have what it takes to be an entrepreneur. * I'm scared new clients will stop booking in. * I'm afraid I'll run out of money and end up on the street. * I'm worried my friends and family will think I'm a failure. * I'm scared of taking big risks. * I'm afraid I'll get haters if I become more visible in my business. * I'm scared I'll get a refund request.

This was one list that was really easy to create. She carried on and on, until there was a whole page of worries, fears and issues. Next, she started using EFT on every one, using a script she'd picked up, and tapping on the meridian sequence that was often used in the videos she'd watched: 'Even though I'm scared I'm not good enough, I deeply and completely love myself.' She repeated the pattern with every single fear on her list. (I created a video for you to help with this, find it at alignandattract.com/eft.) Once she got to the end, she felt a bit light headed. Something was definitely shifting. She gave herself a big shake and did some deep sighing. She was feeling even clearer now. Anna read back through her list. Some of the fears now looked ridiculous. She knew that her husband and family were hardly going to let her end up on the street, and she also knew she'd never let things get that bad. She could see that some of the fears had become habitual ways of thinking, and she could consciously stop those in their tracks if they popped up again. Some of the fears, like maybe getting a hater, or a refund request, could totally happen. In fact, they happen to most people who run an online business at some point. She realised those kinds of fears could really hold her back and she was probably better to instead see herself as a capable person who could handle the situation if it arose. But she could also see that some fears were pretty legitimate. It really did make her feel very insecure to have such uncertainty surrounding her finances. She knew that this insecurity led her to work harder and harder, but that didn't really seem to be helping. And rather than fighting this, and pushing through it, she wondered if there might be another way to create a little more security while she was also focusing on her business. After clearing a lot of the surface fears she'd been swirling in, Anna also found herself acknowledging that she was naturally pretty conservative. Taking big risks just didn't feel good to her. It didn't feel exciting, or exhilarating, or motivating, or bring out her best. Instead, it paralysed her. *Maybe this is a flaw in me,* she thought, *but maybe this is just who I am, and maybe it's okay to accept that. I can take things slower and ensure I feel safe and secure along the way, while continuing to take action. Maybe I can support myself and make things easier for myself.* She didn't really know what supporting herself and allowing things to be easier looked like, yet. But now that she'd acknowledged that she wasn't comfortable with so much financial instability, she could start to address it. Anna took a sigh of relief. She went back to planning her webinar, and now that she was feeling so much more grounded and clear, she found the structure quickly flowed out.

ALIGN + ATTRACT REFLECTION

Your turn: Get out your journal (alignandattract.com/journal) and start a list of your own fears. The more you can come up with, the better! I made an EFT video for you and you can find it at alignandattract.com/eft. Once you have your list, go straight to the page and use the video to get started releasing your fears. Next, go through your list like Anna did and reflect: Which fears are now gone? Which fears are habitual? Which fears are likely to occur, and the answer is to develop your resilience. And which fears are legitimate, and require some more thought, and perhaps action?

STOP BEING A WORKAHOLIC

'I am 100% aligned to trusting myself and life.'

Anna felt so much better after acknowledging the many fears she had. And right now, she was thinking about the number one coping mechanism she had been using to manage that fear: working more. If she was honest about the number of hours she spent working, it was pretty out of control. The truth was, half the time when she was working she was not as focused as she could be. She spent so much time at her laptop that sometimes she felt tired, foggy and demotivated. That slowed her down and meant that the things she really did have to complete took a lot longer. It meant that sometimes, she'd be stuck working in the evenings, feeling frustrated at herself that she could have easily finished the work during normal working hours if she'd focused at the time. Her emails were always open, and she replied right away, whatever the request, and whatever time of day or night the email arrived. Occasionally she didn't really have anything she *had* to do, but instead of logging off and heading outside, or going to a yoga class during the day, reading a book or purposefully taking action on a business building task, she wandered around aimlessly on social media, achieving precisely nothing. Or she'd focus on something meaningless like "researching what others were doing," creating yet another mood board for her brand, or she'd start playing around with the colour or design of her logo, business cards or email signature, as if that was going to somehow grow her business. The truth was, she felt uncomfortable and uneasy when she wasn't working, and worries soon popped up to the surface. In her previous job, she'd worked hard, but there was a pretty good culture around work-life balance. It was unusual if she hadn't left the office by six, same as everyone else. Anna earned the same amount each week whether she had an extremely busy or a quieter working week, and clear KPI's that meant she always knew where she stood. Now there was no one to tell her to stop working, and no consistency of income. Her mode of coping with this seemed to be to work nearly all the time, even if she wasn't being productive, and to feel guilty whenever she wasn't working. She often worked with no plan. She'd get up in the morning and head straight for her computer in her pyjamas, sometimes not eating breakfast or having a shower until hours later. She defaulted to spending time on social media or in her inbox when in doubt about what to do next. At times, she'd forget to have lunch, or make do with toast or some other snack when she was really hungry. She liked the idea of not having to stick to normal working hours but getting up super early for some clients, working until late at night with others and having lots of big gaps during the day seemed to contribute to a feeling of always being half *on*. Plus, she didn't really like working with clients early in the morning or late at night. It was tiring and disrupted her sleep. Anna knew she needed to create some kind of structure for herself so that she knew what her non-negotiable tasks were and where to focus her time and energy. She also needed to take control of her hours, set times that she did want to work with clients, and also make a plan to ensure she always ate lunch, had time to exercise, and knew when she was free to actually relax and take time off. She was going to cut her availability, so she'd only be working one evening a week, and cap how late she worked. No more early mornings. Anna got out a piece of paper and started to draft out a schedule for her week. She chose the days she wanted to focus on seeing clients. She decided on a number of bookings that suited her across the week. And she chose specific client booking times. Only a set number a day and at times that suited her. She knew she wouldn't be able to please all clients by designating times, but also that it was necessary for her own health and the sustainability of her business. She organised her time so that she always had a gap in between clients and a longer break for lunch. She decided she'd always pop outside for at least a quick walk over her lunch break too, planning ahead for meals or picking up lunch at the local health food store on her way. She knew the fresh air and walk would help her focus in the afternoon. She added the times she'd decided upon to her online booking system. Next, she added some designated times to her own online calendar where she'd attend yoga classes or do some other form of exercise. Just assuming she'd fit these things in "sometime" wasn't working, and it felt good to see some structure emerging. She decided that unless she had a client, or had some kind of big deadline, she'd finish up work by 6 pm, same as she used to. She had to admit that although it was theoretically nice to be able to work any hours she chose, she did prefer working during the day and having her nights free. Immediately she was seeing that if she structured her time better, she'd have time for some contract work at her old workplace. They'd raised that as an option in her final weeks. She could see how beneficial it could be for her to have some consistent cash flow right now and with a tighter schedule she knew she could fit it in. She'd use any full days without clients or contract work for business planning, writing, marketing and focusing on those courses she'd signed up for. She also wanted to think about running an online program or workshops. All of this would be much easier to plan with some dedicated time. She decided to trial write a list at the end of each day for the following day, highlighting her three most important tasks so she'd start the day with more focus. She also decided to look up a local co-working space. Maybe she could spend her non-client day there and meet some people in different industries and build her network a little. And she'd also look ahead and arrange in advance to catch up with a business buddy she already knew each week or two, whether for a chat or Skype call. She knew that would help her feel less isolated and more connected.

When Josh got home that night she excitedly shared the decisions she'd made that day and showed him her new schedule. She could see he was genuinely happy for her, but more importantly, she felt proud of herself.

ALIGN + ATTRACT REFLECTION

Your turn! How do you feel about your current work schedule? Would you like to create more structure? Might it be beneficial to cap your workday start or finish times, or restrict the times you schedule appointments? Are you already making time for healthy eating and movement and if not, might you add these to your schedule to ensure they occur? Get out your journal (alignandattract.com/journal) to start making notes and perhaps drafting a new, improved schedule. Are there any weekly or daily commitments you want to add to your own calendar? Are there any changes you want to make to your client scheduling systems if you use these?

LET GO OF PERFECTIONISM

*'I am 100% aligned to accepting
my best is good enough.'*

Anna was thinking about this pattern of perfectionism that had come into sharp focus in her discussion with Josh. She was seeing how it linked back to some of the messages in the letter from her business too: 'Do you want *me* or do you just want more? Bless me, love me and tell me how wonderful I am. Enjoy me and have fun with me.' As she reflected, Anna knew it wasn't just that she always wanted more from her business, she always wanted more from herself too. Far from enjoying the journey she was on to create a successful business, she had a constant hum in the background telling her she wasn't good enough, wasn't smart enough, wasn't helping enough people, wasn't growing fast enough, wasn't doing enough, wasn't working hard enough, wasn't inspiring enough, wasn't earning enough, wasn't enough—full stop. This wasn't a new pattern either; it had always been that way. Wanting more seemed to be a given. Of course she wanted more. Wasn't that why she pursued coaching in the first place? Wasn't that why she started her own business? And yet, she could see how just wanting more and not accepting what she had already created was leading to a great deal of dissatisfaction and a constant feeling of unease. And was it even helping her to create *more* or just driving a sense of impatience and an empty feeling that never filled? She did congratulate herself sometimes; when she'd achieved something. But then she quickly moved onto the next goal or milestone, almost like achieving that goal hadn't been important to her in the first place. 'Enjoy me and have fun with me.' Anna felt perplexed. How did you enjoy something if it wasn't yet successful? Surely you had to focus on working hard to make sure it became successful, and then you could enjoy it more then. Right now, she felt guilty if she had fun. She had so much to do, so far to go. Having fun felt like a ridiculous indulgence, that once again, she could focus on later. After she'd created some more success. She knew she spent a lot of time making sure things were perfect, focusing on little details, writing and re-writing her newsletters, blogs and social media posts and debating the merits of different options of course delivery software, mailing list providers and every other technology tool. Part of her felt like that was just being responsible and diligent, while another, bigger part, knew that it also meant she spent a lot of time busy with insignificant decisions and work that had little impact on her clients, or on the actual success of her business. She felt like her perfectionism had a few benefits. For example, she did want to come across as professional, but the truth was that she'd been working in a corporate environment for years.

She didn't know how not to be professional. So maybe it was time to relax around that. She felt like her perfectionism prevented her making mistakes. However, it also slowed her down and she was starting to realise it was impossible to avoid making mistakes in business anyway, especially when it came to working with technology. As much as Anna had been justifying these attitudes and behaviours, she could see how they really weren't working for her. They were causing her to get bogged down and to think and worry about details that really weren't important in the scheme of things. The more important thing seemed to be taking decisive action. Choosing an option and going with it, and then course correcting as necessary along the way. *What do I really need here?* she asked herself. The answer came right away: *I need to feel safe.* What did THAT mean? She thought about it. Since she was so hard on herself, and criticised herself whenever she made the slightest error, whilst also putting such pressure on herself to also grow and succeed at all costs, she was living in a constant state of fear. And really, this was nothing to do with what anyone else thought or said, or their possible reaction to an error she might make. She had the uncomfortable realisation that she was doing this to herself. That she was actually afraid of her own internal reactions. And her perfectionism was trying to avoid these reactions at all costs with ever-increasing attempts to get everything right. *What do I need to give myself to allow me to feel safer as I continue to grow this business?* she wondered. She began to take notes in her journal: * I give myself permission to experiment and have fun with this business. * I give myself permission to be more decisive and to back my decisions. * I give myself permission to be kind with myself while I'm learning so many new things. * I promise to trust in my own skills and abilities rather than defaulting to self-doubt. * I promise to learn from any mistakes, but to be gentle with myself too. As she carried on listing her promises to herself, and giving herself permission for various things, Anna could feel a calmness and sense of peace arriving that felt quite new, and very welcome.

ALIGN + ATTRACT REFLECTION

Your turn: Do you have any perfectionist tendencies that hold you back? What do you most need to know at the moment? Is there anything you want to give yourself permission for? Any promises you'd like to make yourself to support your growth?

GET CLEAR ON WHO YOU CAN HELP

'I'm 100% clear on who I can help.'

Anna was just off a Skype call with a client. A notification came up in the chat box, 'Such an AMAZING session! Thank you!!! I feel awesome. xx' Anna was smiling; it had been a great session. Jemma was such a fun client. She was totally engaged and came to every session with notes on what had happened between sessions and ready to create more change. Four sessions in, she was already a different person—excited, inspired—talking about the changes taking place at work as she was communicating more effectively and most excitingly, the changes in her relationship as she'd gotten better at talking about her needs and planning for more fun. She'd paid for her series of sessions up front without batting an eyelid at the cost, and had already referred a colleague to work with Anna who had also booked in. The two girls shared what happened in their sessions at a fortnightly coffee catch-up. *She just gets it,* Anna thought, feeling energised and inspired herself. *Imagine if all my clients were like Jemma.* She thought about a few of her other clients. All lovely in their own way, it was true that some of them were kind of hard work. There was Mandy, who constantly changed her session times, often just the day before, right on the borderline of her cancellation policy. There always seemed to be a good reason, but their three-month series of sessions had already stretched to four months and she had several sessions to go. She'd also negotiated a discount on her package at the start, and Anna was so keen to get started, she'd agreed. Mandy seemed to enjoy her sessions, but she certainly didn't have the kind of momentum that Anna was used to seeing with other clients. Anna liked the idea of being flexible, but she wondered how committed to change Mandy really was, and she found that when Mandy's name popped up in her schedule, she was already half-waiting for her to move the appointment. Then there was Penny. Penny loved the idea of working with Anna but was really worried about the cost, the commitment, whether she was going to get results, everything. She'd paid for one session, and enjoyed it, but continued to email with more and more questions about working together longer term and her anxiety around the whole thing was clear. Anna decided in her next email she'd make it clear that it was better to wait until she felt more relaxed around it, and outline some of her other options. Although she was pretty sure Penny would get great results if she did commit, she didn't want to convince someone to work with her. It just didn't feel right. She also had a sneaking suspicion the constant emails would only continue if they did work together. And there was also Lisa. Each session she seemed to get great awareness and would be excited about taking action. Then she'd come to her next session and Anna would ask her what was happening in relation to her goals. Every time the answer would be the same: nothing. She had every excuse under the sun and would vow and declare that this time she really did plan to take action. Anna was an action-taker herself and it was totally perplexing to her. It really felt like she wanted Lisa to achieve her goals a lot more than Lisa herself did. Anna thought about how she felt after her interactions with these clients, which varied from slightly frustrated, to a bit drained. None of these clients were terrible, but compared to her experience working with Jemma, they were showing her some gaps in how she was communicating about the best time to work with a coach, what kind of attitude and approach really supports the process, and what it looks like to be committed to yourself. Anna started to wonder what was it about Jemma that made her so great to work with?

She started a list: * She was ready for change. * She loves the way I work and easily follows all my processes. * She's committed. * She's honest with herself and with me about what's going on. * She knows she's the one who needs to follow through and take action outside of sessions. * She takes responsibility for her progress and does any homework that comes up. * She talks about our work to her friends and colleagues. * She trusts her instincts, she books in quite quickly after reading a few blog posts and is clear I can help her. * She is really interested in personal growth and loves getting recommendations for new books and tools. * She can afford to work with me and is happy with the price. * She wants and needs what I offer and gets great results.

How can I attract more clients like Jemma? Anna wondered. She'd been taught to niche and focus on a specific type of client who fit certain demographics. Whilst it was true that quite a few of her favourite clients were around a similar age and had some really aligned interests, they had very different careers, some were Mum's and some not, some were in relationships and some not, and they originally came to see Anna for different reasons, often because they'd connected to Anna's viewpoint on a particular issue or identified with a problem she'd described. Her ideal clients shared a similar perspective and way of viewing the world and a desire to create positive changes from within. They also had the same kinds of problems; feeling stuck, getting in their own way, over-thinking, putting other people first too much, communication issues, feeling de-motivated or low, and often lacked self-confidence. It was their qualities and how well those matched with the way Anna worked that made a bigger difference to how "ideal" they were, rather than their demographics. It was also true that she didn't just want to work with *anyone*, she wanted to attract more clients who really resonated with the way she worked and how changing their inner world could impact on their external world.

ALIGN + ATTRACT REFLECTION

Your turn: Think about a favourite client. What do you love most about working with this client? What qualities make them ideal for working with you?

SHOW HOW YOU CAN HELP

'I am 100% aligned to communicating how I can help.'

Anna had been thinking about how to connect with more clients just like Jemma. She clicked on her website and opened a new page: 'Is this you?' She began typing, allowing her list and description of Jemma to flow into her writing. She imagined she was writing to Jemma herself before they'd started working together, and what she would have connected to. Soon, she had a great first draft. Next, she thought about how she could bring this into her blog and social media posts. She often wrote about themes she saw with her clients, the kinds of issues her clients came to her with, and lessons she'd worked through in the past. She opened a few blog posts to see if it was clear the kinds of qualities her clients were demonstrating when they worked through these issues, or that she had tapped into herself when overcoming challenges. She also wanted to know if it was clear what kinds of issues she was really great at helping her clients with. Anna had the sense she was on the right track, but as she scrolled, she realised she'd also written quite a few posts she thought might be helpful but that didn't show much of her personality, or in fact, connect to coaching much at all. Posts about yoga, or meditation, or healthy eating, recipes, or generic list posts, which really weren't related to what she worked on with clients. She knew she could be clearer. She also knew that she needed to share her own perspectives more confidently and show more of her true personality, because that would help attract more of her right people. While she was on a roll, she decided to jot down some more ideas to share in blog posts, Lives, webinars or other formats, based on the qualities she really wanted to attract and nurture in her clients, and the themes her clients were often bringing to their sessions. She knew that she really wanted to emphasise the importance of self-responsibility, building your resilience and resourcefulness, being open to possibilities and learning to tune into your own wisdom.

She started her list:

* How to say no (when you're a people-pleaser).

People-pleasing was a big thing for a lot of Anna's clients. They really did want to be kind and compassionate, but then talked about feeling resentful or unable to find time for their own priorities. She had an idea about how to incorporate her thoughts about self-responsibility into this.

* How to commit to yourself.

Anna knew she could include what being committed to yourself looks like when working with a coach as part of this, and she had some other great tips for how to follow through on your goals too.

* What does taking responsibility really mean?

Anna could think of a few conversations she'd had with clients about this and they'd told her it had really clarified this for them. She made a note to ask them if she could share what had come up.

* When is the best time to work with a coach?

Anna knew that a lot of her clients had never worked with a coach and this was the kind of question she was asked quite a lot. She knew that she could include some of the qualities that made Jemma so great to work with in this post.

* How to release overwhelm.

Overwhelm was something that many of her clients described and Anna had some suggestions that she knew had really helped some of her existing clients. This would give her the chance to show how practical her coaching sessions could be. If she did this one as a Live or webinar it could give potential clients a taste of what it was like to work with her.

* How to set goals that you'll actually achieve.

This was something Anna knew she was great at helping others with. She decided that if she did this one as a webinar or video it could double as a resource to send new clients before they started work together.

She had a start. She felt much clearer in what she wanted to communicate. And she knew this was going to make a difference. She was getting more confident in her own knowing about what was right for her in her business.

ALIGN + ATTRACT REFLECTION

Your turn: What kinds of topics might you share about to help educate your clients in how you can help them with particular or work with them? What format would be best for you to do this in? Consider different platforms and modes of delivery, e.g. blog post, e-book, Live broadcasts, webinars, in person events, podcasting or audios, videos, written social media posts, etc. If you're not yet sure, experiment to find what connects with your clients, and be aware that the way people engage obviously changes over time. Keep paying attention to what works for you!

FOCUS ON USEFUL
AND HELPFUL

*'I'm 100% aligned to knowing what is useful
and helpful to my clients.'*

Anna was feeling organised. She had written a blog post based
on one idea, had plans for a video and already conducted a Live
broadcast on her Facebook page based on one of the topics. She was
happy with what she was creating and sharing. She also knew that
it was a big leap for a client to go from reading a blog post or even
watching a video or a Facebook Live to booking in a series of sessions
with her. It felt like something was missing. A lot of Anna's new
clients started working with her because they'd connected in some
way. This was great but given that she wanted to work with more
clients than she currently was, it wasn't quite enough. Anna knew
she needed to find ways for more potential clients to get to know her
and how she could help. As she thought about it she realised that a

lot of her clients had met her in person at an event, they had a mutual contact, or someone she'd worked with already had recommended her. They were mostly women working in corporate environments, and a lot didn't plan to leave their jobs, they just wanted to add more joy and passion into their lives, and that was something she was great at helping them do. *Perhaps, I could run some in person workshops,* she wondered. *With the right topics, I know my clients would love this way of nurturing themselves, and inevitably some will want to work with me afterwards.* The more she thought about it, the more she could see that focusing on creating inspiring and valuable workshops and learning how to market them in ways that connected to her ideal clients was going to have so many benefits. She realised that doing this was going to be SO much more fun and purposeful than focusing her efforts on social media just because it seemed like that's what everyone else is doing. *I have to focus on my own business growth and what feels inspiring and fun for ME,* she decided. She sat down and started brainstorming possible topics and activities she might share in a workshop, paying close attention to what felt the most energising and uplifting to her. She knew that energy would shine through when she started promoting her workshops and would attract the right people. She knew right away that she wanted to focus on the whole experience—lovely nourishing food and teas, a beautiful space, a real focus on nurturing—this was something her clients often said they weren't very good at. Like her, many of them defaulted to working too hard and found it difficult to switch off and take time to do nothing or to look after themselves. *I need to see this as a fun challenge, and an experiment, rather than putting pressure on myself to get a particular outcome. I will soon know if a workshop idea is resonating as I'll get bookings. It's my job to find out what connects for my clients and to keep experimenting until I find what works.*

ALIGN + ATTRACT REFLECTION

Your turn: How can you think outside your current box and create something new for your clients (or customers)? What might feel fun for you to create, and add a lot of value to your clients?

CLEAN UP YOUR MONEY STUFF

'I am aligned to a healthy relationship with my money.'

Anna was looking at her bank account. Being an accountant, she thought the money side of running her own business would be really easy. She'd set up business bank accounts right from the start. She used an online bookkeeping software. And yet, she was surprised to find that the money side of her business was really triggering her. She found not being able to predict her revenue really unsettling. Self-worth stuff was coming up and she found it hard to separate her own worth from the money her business was bringing in. She found herself feeling torn, not wanting to feel greedy and focus excessively on money, but then finding herself even more focused on money as it didn't feel stable enough to allow her to switch off. She thought about her fees. Her coaching school had given some guidelines around what to charge, and Anna had found herself erring on the lower side, believing that this would be more accessible for her clients. This was despite the fact she earned a great salary in her career and brought a lot of expertise from her previous role to her coaching work. When she saw social media posts where people raved about their coach and breakthroughs, she would straight away want to go look at that coach's social media and website. Before she'd been able to stop herself, she'd looked up their pricing, offerings, photos and compared them to her own, even though she knew there was little to gain from this behaviour. She also knew that sometimes she doubted and questioned the value of what she was offering. She fluctuated between seeing huge value, such as when a client made big life changes directly related to their work together, and feeling unsure, especially when a client was slightly slower to create changes in their life or didn't follow through on their action steps between sessions. She was often going overtime in sessions, and she knew this was connected to wanting to offer more and more value, rather than trusting in what she was offering.

If someone told her they couldn't afford to work with her, she felt guilty. Sometimes she did lower her rates to help them out. A few times, clients had later talked about a big holiday they'd booked or how they'd upgraded their wardrobe, or mentioned their large salary in passing. Though Anna was happy for them, it also reminded her she'd assumed they really didn't have the money, when it was more about what they valued or prioritised.

Anna could feel a pang when she heard about coaches charging rates much higher than hers. It made her feel like she should have more confidence and charge more, even though her clients were unlikely to pay that much anyway. She thought about a friend who charged over double what she did, she'd put her rates at that level because her high priced coach had told her too, but it seemed obvious that she just wasn't comfortable with that pricing yet. She was constantly stressed as she had to work really hard to sign up new clients. She wasn't making much money and her confidence was dropping, which seemed to be creating a vicious circle. High rates certainly didn't guarantee a high income. Anna also felt funny when she heard some coaches charged less than her and would momentarily wonder if she'd have more clients if she reduced her rates. She thought of one friend who charged less than she did. She'd just complained recently that she wasn't feeling like some of her clients valued their work together as much as they could, and she was feeling tired and burnt out. That didn't sound like what Anna wanted either. She knew others must go through the same kind of comparison process too. After a discussion with a different friend the other day, Anna noticed that friend had raised her rates to just above what Anna was charging. Anna wondered if she'd been thinking about her clients and what was right for her business when she decided to raise them or whether she'd felt a bit triggered when she found out Anna charged more than she did and that was the driver. Well, she knew the feeling. She couldn't seem to stop comparing either, even though deep down she knew that she had to stop looking at what others were doing and focus on her own business and clientele.

She found herself thinking about her dad's comments when she announced she was going into business, 'It's nice to do something you love but it's hard to make money that way,' and 'You can always go back to accounting when you need to. Job security is important.' He spoke like going back to a "proper job" was the inevitable outcome of her foray into self-employment. She thought about stories her mum had repeatedly shared as they were growing up. Her mum grew up without much money and talked about struggling and the importance of working hard and not taking risks, just in case. Anna tried not to take on her mum's fears but when she got worried about money, it was her mum's voice that she heard. She was aware of her friends continuing along the corporate track, earning bigger salaries and more benefits and talking about their plans to buy property, while she took some steps backwards, for now at least. And she also thought about her peers. In some of the online groups she was in, the conversations about money were quite triggering. People were either talking about huge revenue that felt completely out of reach to Anna, or bemoaning debt, or a lack of clients, or expressing their fears about their money situation. Anna was stuck. She knew enough about the externals of money and budgeting from her accounting background, but it was becoming obvious that some of her internal beliefs and programming were holding her back and preventing her from clearly seeing how to move forwards in her business. She began researching. It was like when she started her business—she had read books, done courses, listened to podcasts and had conversations with other people who had achieved what she was trying to do—now, she needed to do the same with money. Soon she was searching for books and resources on shifting your mindset. She ordered books from Barbara Stanny, Denise Duffield-Thomas, Lisa Nichols and Valorie Burton. She decided to review her rates and make sure they really were right for her at this time. And once she'd really settled on those, she committed to quit the comparison. It just made her question herself. Anna also vowed to continue to look out for examples of people in different industries who had created the kind of businesses she desired; purpose-fuelled, authentic and profitable. She instinctively knew that allowing herself to feel inspired by their success was going to create more positivity, which she could funnel into her own business, and that broadening her horizons and looking at different industries would be so helpful. She also knew there was a world of difference between being inspired and simply trying to copy what others were doing and how they were doing it. That may have been tempting earlier on but now it wasn't even a consideration.

ALIGN + ATTRACT REFLECTION

Your turn: How do you feel about your current fees/pricing, do they feel at the right level? Is it time to evaluate these and perhaps make changes in line with what's best for you, your clients and your business? Have any money stories from your childhood or that you've heard parents or other important adults in your life tell impacted on how you feel about money now? Have you read any books on changing your mindset around money or success lately? Might it help to do some further reading now?

PUT BOUNDARIES
IN PLACE

'I am 100% aligned to healthy boundaries.'

Anna had just finished up a client session. She'd gone over time, again, but this time by nearly thirty minutes. She sometimes found it hard to wrap up, she had so much she wanted to share with her clients, and she really wanted them to get great results. But this was ridiculous. It was totally linked to how she valued her time and energy. In her previous job, she hadn't experienced this. She always stuck to time. These days, sometimes her clients messaged her through Facebook Messenger or other social channels at night or on the weekends, and she found herself feeling obliged to respond right away. She never would have done that in her old job. Some of her coaching clients emailed her between sessions to ask questions. Back when she just had a few clients, this really didn't bother her and long backwards and forwards conversations would ensue. Now she was becoming much busier and the requests and questions were becoming more frequent. In her old work, this wasn't even a consideration. Other times, clients who were also acquaintances or industry friends started casual conversations with her that ended up feeling a bit like free coaching. The lines felt blurred. Of course she wanted to be able to chat, but she didn't really want to create one-sided friendships where she was seen as the go-to person to talk through issues in her personal time. Sometimes these conversations stretched on for hours. Of course she knew a lot about what was going on for them, as that was what they focused on in their sessions, but they didn't know much of what was going on for her. In most cases a friendship beyond knowing each other socially hadn't existed prior to the client relationship, and this didn't feel like the way to create a balanced one. Occasionally, personal issues came up in conversations with colleagues in her previous work place and with the odd client, but the boundaries had felt much clearer. Sometimes she'd also get long emails from readers and social media followers connected to something she'd posted about and sharing a long story of how it had resonated and why. She was glad to be connecting, but it didn't feel appropriate to get into a long backwards and forwards conversation as had occasionally happened, especially when the individual wasn't actually interested in booking in for coaching and just wanted to share. She knew she needed to get clearer on how to handle this. Her pre-coaching friends had always enjoyed the fact that she was a great listener and asked a lot of questions, but now she was becoming aware that in some cases, she was starting to feel more like a coach or counsellor in her relationship with them too. She slipped into her coaching role a little too easily. With a few friends, this had started to mean that conversations often centred around problem-solving whatever the latest issue was in their lives. Again, this didn't feel balanced. A couple of friends rarely asked what was going on for her anymore. They might love having the listening ear, but what was she actually getting out of these kinds of relationships?

Anna's phone pinged. It was Josh, checking in about her day and also asking if she wouldn't mind picking up something at the shops for him if she was out and about, and could she drop off his dry cleaning if she had time. This was happening more and more often. Since she worked from home, Josh sometimes assumed that she had more time to do home-related tasks, forgetting that she was actually focused on her business during the day; she was working. He never used to ask these kinds of questions when she was working in an office. Sometimes friends or family members also assumed she had plenty of time on her hands during the day too, a situation that Anna had no doubt contributed to in the earlier days. Back then her days had way less structure and she was probably looking for distractions too. These are all boundary problems, Anna was realising. In most cases, easily rectified by getting clear on what she really wanted and needed herself and sticking to it. In other cases, by being willing to have a loving and clear conversation about what she was noticing. And in some cases, the issue could be easily managed by being clearer in the way she responded. With Josh, she could explain to him why she wasn't able to do home-related tasks during the day, unless something urgent came up. And then, if he forgets, she could just reiterate that she was working, and it would have to be done later. With clients, she was the one responsible for time-management and she had to start wrapping up her calls five or ten minutes or so before the end and let the client know this was happening, so they could include last-minute comments or questions then, rather than right at the end. When questions came in between sessions, she might sometimes answer quick ones, but let them know she'd noted other questions to work through in their next session. And when she received those long emails or messages, she could offer thanks and a brief validation, and also let them know if they ever wanted to work on the issue more deeply with her that they were very welcome to book in a session and she'd provide a link to book. Compassionate and clear. With friends, she'd need to be sensitive, but she knew she needed to be less available to work through issues. She had to pay attention to what she was receiving, as well as giving to the friendship, and invest her time and energy into relationships where there was a more equal balance. Collectively, she knew that doing these things would make a big difference to how she was feeling in her business.

ALIGN + ATTRACT REFLECTION

Your turn: Are you experiencing any boundary challenges in your own business in relation to your time, energy, or communication? Are there any changes you'd like to make? Are there any conversations you need to have to assist with this process?

COME INTO YOUR OWN ENERGY

'I am 100% aligned to staying in my own energy.'

Anna closed down her emails. She'd had a positive few days. Turns out putting boundaries around her time and energy and releasing some of the fears that had been holding her back was actually making a difference. She'd slept through the previous night; for the first time in ages not waking once. She knew that was probably because she'd started actually switching off in the evenings. Last night she and Josh had a glass of wine together as they prepared dinner and danced around the kitchen with the music turned up loud like they always used to do. After that she'd put her phone away and read a book, something she hadn't done in … well, so long ago that she couldn't remember when. She'd unfollowed a bunch of social media accounts, especially those that seemed to give her an anxious, not-enough feeling, along with a lot of people in her industry. She knew that had been contributing to her feelings that the market was saturated, and probably influencing what she was posting about herself. It was all part of taking control and ensuring she stayed focused on her own life and business. She'd even had a new client book in, who told her she loved following her on social media and liked her latest blog post about finding joy, telling her, 'It was just what I needed to hear.' In that moment, Anna had felt elated. But right now, she was feeling dejected. A different client had just emailed to cancel her next session and told her she couldn't afford to continue sessions at the moment. Anna immediately filled with doubt. She felt a pang at her heart; a feeling of heartbreak. Thoughts started to crowd her mind, *I probably wasn't helping her enough, maybe I'm charging too much, I should be doing more. What if other clients pull out? What am I doing wrong, is this just an excuse and she doesn't like me, maybe I should offer her a discount?* Anna felt herself spiralling. This roller coaster of emotions was constant. If something good happened in her business, she felt great, invincible even. If something bad happened in her business, even something simple like unsubscribes, lost likers, a questioning comment, a client cancelling a session, she crashed. Hard. Sometimes in multiple cycles in one day. Not only that, she felt totally responsible for the progress her clients made. When things started moving forwards for them, she was excited, yes, but mostly relieved. Surely this meant she was doing a good job. Her clients told her how much they looked forward to their sessions and got excited sharing the changes they were making, but somehow it never felt like quite enough. The doubt remained. She felt constant, unrelenting pressure to make sure her clients had huge breakthroughs, deep insights and that they backed these up with tangible changes. She all but went and made the changes for them, and would have done that too, if it were possible. It was exhausting.

She got out her journal and wrote a question: 'What is going to happen if I keep doing this?' She wrote in dot points: * I will end up exhausted. * I will hate my business. * I will resent my clients. * I will end up back at my old job. * I will always be on a roller coaster with all my moods dictated by what's happening for my business and clients.

She let out a deep sigh and rested her head in her hands. This felt horrible. How could she make it stop? She'd been doing so well and had been a lot kinder to herself since her realisation that she'd essentially been making life impossible for herself with her perfectionism and incessant focus on more. But now she could feel her positivity slipping. Another question formed in her mind and she wrote it down: 'What beliefs would support me right now?' Another list started: * I am always doing the best I can, and that's enough. * I can feel happy whatever is going on for my business and my clients. * It is safe for me to allow my clients to take responsibility for their own choices and actions. * All of my clients are on their own path and I am just one part of their journey. * I am always supportive and loving towards myself as I grow my business.

She sighed deeply, this time with relief. *What would be different if I supported myself, even when things feel like they're not working, or something goes wrong?* she mused. *I can't even imagine how much easier things would be. Maybe I should try it, just for a change,* she was laughing by the last point. *I'm going out for a walk round the park, my next client isn't for a couple of hours now and I need to let this settle,* she decided. She opened her emails to check them before setting off. There was a new client enquiry. *Nice one,* she thought. *Can't wait to help. I'll reply as soon as I'm back from my walk.* She closed her laptop and headed out the door.

ALIGN + ATTRACT REFLECTION

Your turn. Get out your journal and reflect: Do you notice a rollercoaster of emotions affecting you in your business? What causes you to feel elated, and what causes you to crash? What negative effects might occur if your own cycle continues? What beliefs might support you in your business right now? Write your own list of supportive beliefs you'd like to reinforce.

BACK YOURSELF

'I'm 100% aligned to backing myself.'

Anna had just finished a morning back at her old accounting firm. They'd gladly welcomed her back for a contract related to a client she already had a great relationship with. It was part-time and for just three months, but only a week in, there was already talk she might take on another contract after this ended. Either way, Anna felt comfortable keeping her options open at this point. She could already see how the reduced financial pressure was improving her approach to working in her business. She was taking consistent action, blogging, doing social media posts and Facebook and Instagram live videos about themes her clients were talking to her about. She'd scheduled a webinar too, about how to find your joy when you're feeling bored and stuck, something new clients often told her they felt. She was feeling much clearer herself, and since she'd started having fun again outside of business and work, she'd noticed that she had more personal insights to share and ideas for things to write about and share. She found herself thinking more about the clients she loved working with and what would help them rather than her own doubts and insecurities. That morning a colleague had casually asked how her new business was going as they walked to a meeting together.

"Yeah, good," she'd replied. "Still in the early stages but it's going well."

Once, she would have worried at looking like a failure to her old colleagues. She'd been so excited and optimistic as she finished up. Now she didn't care. Things in the business were progressing just fine. And this was a good choice for now. She didn't feel any need to justify her decisions or attach her worth to anyone else's opinion. And it fit with one of her big picture goals: 'I want to live and work in ways that feel sustainable and expansive.' Right now, this option was making her business feel more sustainable and she felt really comfortable with that. In fact, she'd had multiple conversations in the past few weeks that reflected her new attitude. Her mother had expressed concern about whether she had enough money on the phone the other day. 'You don't need to worry about me, Mum,' she'd told her firmly. 'Starting a new business is something people do every day and I'm doing fine. I'm on track and making money. You are going to have to find something else to stress about, sorry.' They'd both laughed at the last comment. Anna's mum was known throughout the family as an incessant worrier. She also caught up with her brother.

"Are you still doing that hippy stuff?" he asked.

"What, coaching? Thinking about what you want to do and how you want to live your life and changing your mindset is hardly a hippy thing to do. In fact, I think you could use a coach. I could coach you right now. Where shall we begin, with your approach to a loss at the football perhaps? Whaattt, I can totally help!" she threw up her hands, giggling as he retreated.

"What football team?" he groaned.

And with that, the topic was changed, as he'd lamented the coach, the umpires and the injuries rife in his team. Even conversations with her husband were now different, as she deliberately switched off from work in the evenings. She gave him the highlights of her day and then they talked about other things. In recent weeks they'd been out for a mid-week movie, to a local pub jazz night, and went down the beach for a walk and fish and chips. None of these events even made it onto social media. She'd caught up with some girlfriends for coffee; friends who didn't have businesses. Previously she'd enthusiastically shared details of her new life, and although they were happy for her, it was apparent they didn't really understand the coaching world that she was so immersed in. This time she happily gave a very brief overview and focused more on what she and Josh had been up to. The other girls didn't try to sell their career choices to her and she didn't need to sell coaching to them either. Back when she'd been desperate for everyone else's approval, it seemed like everyone had an opinion on her business. And she'd taken every one of those opinions on; worrying, stressing, justifying and defending her position. Now that she shut these conversations down before they went too far, she felt a sense of freedom. Some people asked her about her business from a place of true curiosity, or had a business of their own, and a useful opinion to share or insight to offer. She happily engaged in those conversations and shared more deeply. But she'd realised that sharing details of her business with friends and family who had no real interest in or understanding of business variously brought up their own fears of being in such a position, bored them, confused them or led to her going around in circles trying to explain what she did and why she was doing it. All too often she found herself trying to win their approval or gain validation. It just wasn't necessary, she'd concluded. There was a sense of relief in knowing she could share the highlights and leave the other conversations for her business friends.

ALIGN + ATTRACT REFLECTION

Your turn: Is the way you talk about your business supportive of your goals? Do you ever find yourself selling your current life choices to friends or family? Are there any changes you want to make in your communication? Are there any new boundaries you want to put in place?

RECOGNISE YOUR OWN PROGRESS

'I'm 100% aligned to staying on my own path and recognising my progress.'

When Anna had started her business, it had been such a challenge to find the right tone in her writing. She was used to a relatively formal and corporate style of communication in her workplace. That didn't feel right for her business. And yet it also didn't feel right to be too casual. Using terms of endearment like gorgeous, beautiful, babe or goddess in her communication wasn't really her, although many of her peers felt comfortable being really personal like this. There had been a shift though. Now that she was so focused on communicating and connecting with her ideal clients, she felt more comfortable just being herself, rather than getting caught up in how she should sound. She was getting clearer on what she wanted to share on social media. Certainly, she was sharing a lot more of her own thoughts now, and always thinking about her clients and what she wanted to communicate and share with them. She was happy to be getting more engagement on social media, and her accounts were slowly growing. When she worked with clients, they quite often referenced things she'd written about on social media. Her posts were certainly resonating. The more she'd focused on connecting and the less she's worried about learning rules, or tricks, or worrying about what was or wasn't happening with algorithms, the clearer her message had become. That was being reflected back to her quite tangibly now, both with engagement, and with clients booking in for coaching and the workshop she'd just run. In the end, ten people had signed up for Anna's workshop. She was happy with that! She'd worked hard on creating a workshop her clients would find useful and nurturing and providing a wonderful experience. Some of her existing clients came and ads had worked really well at attracting new people. A couple had already gone on to book in some coaching sessions with her, with others saying they planned to down the track. She was already planning her next workshop. Still, it often didn't feel "enough". She couldn't help but notice that some of her peers and the people she admired had much bigger followings. Sometimes, she felt frustrated. Why wasn't she growing faster? Maybe her message wasn't "big" enough. Maybe it wasn't powerful enough. She'd find herself thinking that she was missing something. Sometimes she found herself getting a little fixated. She'd share a blog post and pay way too much attention to how many likes that post got, or how many people it reached. She'd worry about how to get new people to sign up to her newsletter, and what else to try for a free opt-in. Lately, she had been obsessing about her subscriber numbers and how to grow them. She was writing to her subscribers consistently, and got nice responses back from nearly every newsletter, but it somehow didn't feel like enough. Why were the numbers climbing so slowly when she put so much effort into it? Her last webinar had fifty people sign up. That was an improvement on the seven who had signed up for her first webinar, but also hardly felt groundbreaking. How was she going to get more people to engage with her content? How was she going to grow her reach? She let out a sigh of frustration. Her mobile rang. It was Alexa. As they chatted, the conversation turned to business, and Alexa asked about Anna's webinar.

"I saw lots of comments about it on social media," she told Anna. "You're doing so well, people love your stuff."

Anna started to tell her that actually, she'd only had 50 sign up for the call, and she really thought she should be doing better, when Alexa chimed in, "50?! Oh, my God, that's so good! I really should do a webinar. But it all feels way too hard."

She went on to explain she never knows what to say, she didn't know what her message was, that she wasn't techy and that it probably wouldn't work, that she couldn't decide on the best platform to use, and that she probably wouldn't get anything like 50 on the call, maybe she'd get 5, and what was the point of all that effort for 5 people? As Anna listened, she had the uncomfortable realisation that this was exactly like the conversation she'd just been having in her own head. Sure the numbers were different, and the source of the angst had changed, but she had been turning herself into the same ridiculous knots.

Anna found herself saying, "The thing is, you just have to start somewhere. If you don't want to do a webinar, choose something else. Maybe a workshop is better for you. But if you decide to run a webinar and only 5 sign up, that might still be great too, especially if you really help those people solve a problem they have right now."

She went on to explain that sure, she only had 7 sign up to her first webinar, but one of those people had become a client, and she'd used the webinar as a free opt-in gift for a while afterwards, and it got some lovely feedback. She'd really thought about the content for the webinar and based it on a theme lots of her clients had been talking to her about. She made sure the webinar was practical and that her viewers would go away feeling empowered and inspired. And the techy stuff, well, having some kind of issues was probably inevitable at some stage. Everyone experiences tech issues, no point letting it hold you back. Alexa didn't sound convinced, and Anna knew she was more than likely going to put off taking action on it for a good while yet. The conversation soon moved on to a different topic. As Anna hung up the phone a short time later, she had to recognise that despite her "slow" progress, she was indeed making progress. She was getting out of her own way and showing up consistently. Rather than getting caught up in excuses and coming up with reasons why things were difficult or not worth doing, she was experimenting, and she was refining her message. She wasn't getting stuck in the thinking and analysing phase like she used to. The webinar with 50 people did get a lot of feedback and quite a few comments on social media. She only got one further client from that webinar, but there was no doubt her people were engaged, and she was getting more and more chances to refine her message and become known as someone who could help with particular issues and problems. The only real "problem" was arising when she started comparing her progress to other people's, or when she got hooked into seeking validation from numbers or likes. In that moment, she remembered an industry colleague who she'd admired with a huge online following being shocked when Anna had told her the number of clients she was currently working with. The colleague didn't have any clients at the time. She'd decided attracting clients was too hard and had instead focused on working with brands as an influencer but wasn't making much money from that yet. It had been a bit of a reality check, and Anna had wondered how many other people she perceived to do be doing so much better than her really were. Equally, she knew of some people who were too busy working in their business, and making money, to devote much time or energy to social media or to appear outwardly successful. Either way, she knew it was a waste of time and energy thinking about it. She had to stay focused on what she was creating herself. Maybe the problem wasn't Anna's numbers. And it wasn't her message. Maybe it was about what she was choosing to focus on and learning to accept the speed and flow of her own unique path. Anna was noticing and continuing to build on what WAS working for her and letting go of worrying about what other people were doing or how she compared.

ALIGN + ATTRACT REFLECTION

Your turn: What kinds of things do you notice yourself becoming attached to? In what ways have you noticed yourself comparing what you're doing to what others are doing and judging yourself unfavourably? Where do you currently find yourself getting caught up in knots? What progress or outcomes would you like to acknowledge at this time?

RESPECT YOUR PRIVILEGE

'I am aligned to being inclusive.'

Anna was at a casual catch up with a group of business friends and she was seated next to two women she didn't know. Rosie was wrangling a small child in between drinking her coffee, and Gabrielle was sharing about her copywriting business; she did most of her writing for a couple of large corporate clients, and also did some freelance book editing on the side. Anna was fascinated and asked lots of questions. Someone from the group had picked up Rosie's child and was reading him a story and Rosie finally had the chance to join in the conversation.

"What's your business, Rosie?" Anna asked her.

"I make websites," Rosie shared. "But that's just at night. I work in retail during the day, then pick up Jonas from childcare and start on the websites after he goes down for the night. Usually

I work til around 11 or 12 and then I go to bed and start all over again the next day."

"Wow, that is so dedicated," Anna shared. "You must be exhausted. I used to work nights but then I stopped because I felt like I was getting out of balance."

"Yeah I am pretty much always exhausted," Rosie agreed. "But it's just me and Jonas and I want us to have a great life, so that's what I do." She was completely matter of fact about it.

Anna was shocked. "You look after your baby by yourself, you work all day and then you work half the night too? You are amazing!"

"And, Jonas usually wakes at least once or twice overnight as well. It's pretty constant."

Anna's eyes were wide. Her own efforts to create *balance* now seemed somewhat trivial and indulgent despite the fact she knew they were still necessary. She didn't have children, she had the support of a loving husband, and she was able to make choices about when she worked and how many hours she worked. She did worry about failure, but her back up was going back to work full-time in a professional job. Thinking about Rosie's situation was giving her a healthy dose of perspective. The conversation had turned to social media. Gabrielle was sharing how she'd been blocked on Facebook for a period after calling out a series of racist comments on her page in response to discussions she'd started about a recent event. Her post was setting boundaries around the type of engagement she welcomed on her page and what she'd no longer tolerate, but it was deleted, and she was blocked.

Anna was gobsmacked. "You called out some racist comments and YOU were blocked? But that doesn't make any sense."

"Yeah, it infuriates me, but that's what happens. It has

happened to friends too, but not my white friends. There sure are different rules for different people. It's a constant challenge."

Anna felt uncomfortable as she realised she didn't know how things differed in the online world for her friends who weren't white.

"Oh, my God, Gabrielle, that completely sucks. What else is different?" she asked.

"Well for a start, have you noticed how many telesummits and podcasts feature nearly exclusively white guests? Or how many people talk about empowerment, but really, they're talking about the empowerment of women just like themselves, which is often white, young, straight, middle-class, attractive—yet, when I get empowered and speak out, I get freaking blocked on Facebook—it's just not a level playing field. Not to mention the white centring and white fragility that occurs when people are called out on their non-inclusive or downright racist ways. I could go on, but it gets pretty tiring. There are a ton of indigenous, black and coloured people out there educating on this topic though. To be honest, sometimes the most harm comes from ignorance. People say things they think are neutral like 'I don't see colour,' 'I just focus on love, or being positive,' or 'I don't want to get political,' blah blah blah. It completely misses the point. Some of us don't have that privilege."

Anna was nodding. "Gabrielle, I really had no idea, thanks for sharing all this. I totally need to follow up and learn more."

Anna could feel herself getting slapped in the face with even more perspective. She had privilege that she was often completely blind to. She too was guilty of assuming that others hit up against similar kinds of challenges she did when in reality, many were facing far deeper and often invisible barriers that no amount of empowerment pep talks were going to immediately resolve. She'd read excellent articles from Layla Saad and other resources, but there was clearly more to think about and learn. When Anna left the catch up, for once she wasn't feeling worried or anxious about what she was or wasn't doing in her business. She was filled with respect for women like Rosie and Gabrielle who were hitting up against far bigger barriers than she faced and breaking through them, too. More than that, she felt a sense of responsibility. *Whether I acknowledge it or not, I am privileged,* she was realising. *It's pretty unlikely I'm going to be shut down on Facebook for sharing an opinion or setting boundaries. People who look like me are easy to find in summits and on podcasts and everywhere else online. I have a loving partner who could financially support me for a while if it came to that. I have a supportive family and grew up with a lot of stability. I have a university education and could afford to take coaching training and choose a career change.* It wasn't about feeling guilty for her circumstances. But she could be more aware. Anna committed to remembering to ask herself: 'How could I be more inclusive? Am I considering other perspectives and experiences? And what am I doing to continue to learn?' That night, she looked up Layla Saad's articles and noted she needed to talk to white women about white supremacy part 1 and 2, absorbing the education and call to action, and started to go deeper with some of the other resources she recommended. She ordered a couple of books online: *So You Want to Talk About Race* by Ijeoma Oluo and *Why I'm No Longer Talking to White People About Race* by Reni Eddo-Lodge, and signed up to a couple of Patreon accounts by women educating on racism.

She next went through her website and blog post archives, paying close attention to the images she'd chosen. Were they inclusive? She felt uncomfortable as she realised that nearly all the images were of white, skinny women in their twenties. So, not inclusive at all. *Ugh.* She hadn't even realised until now, even though, her clients certainly weren't all white, thin and in their twenties. She immediately began a search on a stock photo website for images that better represented the people she worked with—different sizes, ages, skin tones and ethnicities.

She knew she still had a lot of work to do to unpack her blind spots and to be more inclusive. It was a start.

ALIGN + ATTRACT REFLECTION

Your turn: Do you have any inbuilt advantages that you may not have acknowledged, whether due to race, education level, class, sex, your family, the country you were born, the support you have around you, or anything else? This is not an invitation to feel guilty or defensive, but instead an opportunity to powerfully acknowledge any privilege you experience, and potentially gain a new perspective to do your own further learning so you aren't inadvertently causing harm, and if desired, to answer the question Anna poses in your own way: How could I be (even) more inclusive?

STAY IN YOUR OWN LANE

'I'm 100% aligned to staying in my own lane.'

Anna was at a business and blogging conference. Some of her friends from coaching school and contacts she'd made through online courses and social media were there too. In the lunchtime break, conversation naturally turned to business and what everyone was doing. Anna heard about Dana's new podcast and all the amazing guests she was interviewing. Podcasts were so popular. She started to wonder if she should think about creating one herself. Kate had a book deal with a publisher. Anna had always assumed she'd eventually write a book. She planned to self-publish to give herself more freedom. But having a publisher did sound so impressive. She began to doubt herself. Lana had employed a PR agency and was getting some mainstream media mentions in magazines and newspapers, and a few speaking gigs too. Was this Anna's next step? Shima had joined an expensive mastermind and was excited about the contacts she was making and the new strategies she was learning. Anna couldn't help feeling like she was missing out and being left behind. Sian was investing in an online business team who were setting up funnels and systems for her and managing her Facebook ads to grow her list. That sounded kind of smart. Was that where she should invest next? Marion was growing a big free group which took a lot of her time, but she hoped it was going to lead to more paid clients. Maybe that was a sensible idea? And then there were the actual speakers and panellists. Stories of big launches, sponsorship deals, fast growing mailing lists, speaking at international conferences, travel, sales funnels, successful online courses, corporate gigs and impressive results. Even though Anna had started focusing more on her own business and was trying to avoid comparing herself to others, hearing all these stories in person was triggering her. Again. She sighed. Not only that, she was thinking about her conversation with Gabrielle. Nearly all the panellists and speakers she'd seen so far had been white; there was very little diversity and that was reflected in the perspectives presented. She felt uncomfortable knowing that she may not have even noticed that previously, but she was paying a lot more attention after that conversation. And the speakers were mostly men too. Sure, she'd say something on the feedback form, and offer some suggestions for great speakers from diverse backgrounds to invite in future, but shouldn't she be doing more. As everyone started to gather to go in for the next speaking session, Anna decided she needed to step outside for a few minutes to gather her thoughts. She took some deep breaths of fresh air. Her mind was racing. She had a headache. She was completely overwhelmed. There were so many options for how she could move forwards in her business.

How could she possibly make the right choice? Not only that, but she felt completely inadequate. She felt like the tiniest fish in the biggest ocean. Like she was never going to have any impact or be seen or heard. She'd temporarily forgotten all about her own clients and audience; the people she was actually having an impact on. She was caught up in comparison and it was making her feel like a complete failure. Anna could feel her thoughts and emotions spiralling downhill like they regularly used to do in the early days of her business. She knew where that would lead. She knew she had to stop the downward spiral now and she needed to manage her own reaction to the new ideas and information she was receiving. *I have to get back in my own lane,* she reminded herself. *I am enough. I am doing enough. I am growing fast enough. My business is good enough. I am on the right track. And I will continue to make great choices for me.* For now, she decided to list down all the different ideas and potential pathways that had sparked her interest, curiosity or jealousy: * Podcast. * Book deal. * PR. * Speaking. * Mastermind. * Online business team. * Funnels. * Facebook ads. * Mailing list. * Corporate events. * Workshops. * Online course. * Group program. * Free group. Of course, she couldn't and wouldn't do all of them, but the fact they had caused her to question herself meant it would be useful to examine each more closely later and analyse how they might fit with her own goals. Not now. Not while she was in her current mental space. She knew she had to re-connect to her own priorities before she thought more about each option. She had to think about her own evolving business model, and the smartest ways to achieve her goals. With that, Anna headed back inside and re-joined the conference.

ALIGN + ATTRACT REFLECTION

Your turn: Specific strategies and approaches are always changing. What's on your radar right now? Where might you invest time and/or money to grow your business? Create your own list of options.

TAKE ACTION BASED ON YOUR PRIORITIES

'I am 100% aligned to my own priorities.'

Anna was reflecting on the conference and the long list of strategies and approaches she might invest in to grow her business. She knew that any one of the options that had inspired her at the conference worked beautifully for some people, but that she needed to think about her own goals and what would fit best with those. She was aware that some of the ideas she'd heard sounded impressive, but that didn't mean they were actually a good fit for her own business right now. Some ideas sounded fun, or would help her meet lots of cool people, but those weren't really her highest priorities. Other ideas involved a big investment of time with the hope there would be a payoff later.

She knew she'd have to be very strategic if she wanted to go down that route or she could end up with a lot more work to do, and no real benefit to her business. There were also plenty of ways she could throw big sums of money at her business in the hope that would lead to growth, but she also knew that investing big sums didn't guarantee a return, and that she needed to be clear about what she invested in and why. She also knew she could easily get tempted to try a number of new things and soon her energy (and bank account) would be more depleted and scattered than ever. Just because there were a lot of options, it didn't mean they'd all actually help her grow the size or impact of her business. Anna reminded herself that following formulas had never really worked for her. She knew that just following someone else's steps to success was not going to work if she didn't have clarity about what she really wanted. It was time to reconnect to her own bigger picture and identify her priorities.

She wrote three headings at the top of pages in her journal: 'What's working well in my business? What's not working well and what gaps can I see? What's my next step?' As Anna started writing about what was working well in her business, she recognised she was attracting some great clients. Her boundaries were so much better, and she was communicating really well. The list of what wasn't working so well was a little longer. She felt like she was spending way too much time on social media and that growing her following and getting interaction was getting harder, if anything. Even authentic posts that used to get lots of interaction were hardly being seen now, and ads weren't working like they once did either. Her business had just one main income stream, her clients, along with the occasional workshops she ran. And she was mostly attracting those clients through social media, along with some referrals. She looked at her notes. *So, I only have one main income stream and that is coming mostly through one channel, social media, and I feel like that's only getting harder. Okay then!* She moved onto her third question. She revisited her list from the conference and was able to immediately eliminate most of the options now that she'd spent a short time thinking about her own business and priorities. It was clear to her that at this time she needed an additional income stream. And she didn't want it to be reliant on social media. That eliminated some further options from her list. *Corporate events, hmmm.* This wasn't something she'd considered yet, but all of a sudden it was standing out as a good next step. She did enjoy running her workshops, and perhaps this would be a way of expanding on that. She decided she would talk to Ju and Claudine. They both worked in HR. They might be able to give Anna some clues about how to approach organisations about running a wellness program. Maybe something on stress-relief, or resilience, or mindfulness. She'd have to talk to some of her friends and ask if they've participated in any kind of wellbeing programs at work and how they worked and what they feel is needed. As she continued to think about it, a new pathway started to emerge: *I could package a workshop with an online class or course guiding people through some skills related to what I teach in the workshop. And I could include an individual coaching session, or series of sessions for each participant as part of the package too. I could offer several options for support, from a simple workshop and the online program up to a longer term coaching arrangement around specific goals and outcomes.* Anna was starting to feel excited. This would be such a good use of her time and skills and could help so many people! She could suddenly see how this kind of approach could potentially solve a number of issues at once. A new and abundant income stream, yes, but also a different marketing pathway, and perhaps even a new avenue for attracting ongoing clients. *Okay! This is great. But I'm going to have to be SO clear about how I approach companies, how I package the program up and how I communicate the value to each company. I'll have to really think about the outcomes and benefits, so it feels very tangible.* There was a ton to think about and work on, but Anna was feeling inspired. *What would be a really quick and simple way to test whether this idea might work and help me develop it further?* she wondered. Anna immediately thought of her sister-in-law's vet clinic. Maha had talked about wanting to improve the culture amongst staff and create a more positive environment. She decided to call Maha tonight and talk to her about running a pilot version of the workshops and a follow up coaching session for each staff member if they wanted that too. She could test her idea, get feedback, and if it all worked well, ask for a testimonial, which she knew would be invaluable when she started approaching other companies. She'd also start on her other research activities by talking to Ju and Claudine and other friends, but she didn't want to get stuck in research mode. It felt like the best way to find out how her idea would work was to test it in on a small scale the real world.

ALIGN + ATTRACT REFLECTION

Your turn: Go to your journal and start jotting notes under the headings: What's working well in my business? What's not working well and what gaps can I see? What's my next step? Refer back to your own list of the options that you might use to grow your business. Based on your own reflections, which options feel like a good fit for you right now? Is there any further research you might do? What actions can you immediately take?

FIND WHAT WORKS FOR YOU

'I am aligned to finding my own solutions and staying on my own path.'

Anna was at a coaching meet up. She knew quite a few people there. In some cases, they already knew each other from previous in person events, studying together, or online connections, and in other cases they were meeting for the first time, recognising each other from pictures shared on social media. So many of her coaching friends were really positive and it was inspiring hearing about the different ways they were each moving forward. There was the opportunity to have a vent about challenges with people who understood as well.

"I'm so stressed," Monica confided. "I haven't had a new client book in for weeks, and lots of my clients are finishing up. I have no idea what I'm going to do next."

Anna was totally honest, "I have felt like that before. It was insanely stressful!"

She explained how she looked into all her options and carried on taking action in her business but also took a part-time contract back at her old work. She shared how awesome it was not to be stressing about money, and how her business had been growing steadily since then. She thought it was probably because the pressure was off, and she didn't feel desperate and clients could feel that.

"I thought about doing that," Monica replied, "But it felt like failure. I want to show the Universe I'm serious about this business. I don't want to send mixed messages."

"You know … you don't need to put that kind of pressure on yourself if you don't want to. I feel like way more of a success now that I'm not freaking out about money all the time, trust me," Anna laughed.

Monica looked unsure. Across the room Anna saw Lisa. They'd been following each other online for a while and recently Anna had gotten the uncomfortable feeling that Lisa was getting a little TOO inspired by some of her stuff. She'd been sharing posts on some of the same themes Anna was writing about, and sometimes even using some of the same phrases. Something had made her click through to Lisa's site the other day and she couldn't believe it when she saw that one of the pages on her site was almost a direct copy of her own. She'd just changed around some wording. *Ugh.* Anna decided to avoid talking to her; she had no idea what to say. She was soon in a conversation with Rahda who was talking about live events she was running to bring new clients into her business. There was a whole formula to the process, right down to the sales script she used at the end of the workshop and follow up calls to each participant, which also followed a set script. Rahda said she'd been tired of trying to figure it all out on her own so decided to learn from "the best" and was paying a hefty five figure sum to do so.

"Sounds great," Anna affirmed. "So long as you're enjoying it and it's working for your business, why not?"

Rahda hesitated and then shared that she actually kind of hated the formula; it felt very rigid. Most of the time participants avoided her calls. And truth be told, it wasn't really working yet. The process had brought in two new clients from her two workshops, which was something, but the workshops themselves were quite tiring and expensive to run. Not to mention the cost of the coaching itself. She was counting on sales to keep covering her payments.

"I think it will get easier though, the coach said that if I skip any steps of the formula I won't get results, so that's what I'm focusing on. I just need to get better at following the formula. I know it will work. It has to work. This coach is the best of the best and she says it works. I need to be patient."

Anna couldn't help noticing there was a forced positivity in Rahda's tone. Anna thought about her own workshops. The way she was doing them wasn't necessarily putting her on the path to riches, but also felt fun and light, and they were profitable. She also hadn't spent over 10k upfront before running them and felt completely free to experiment with different approaches, as she wasn't tied to any formula. She obviously didn't bring that up. Another friend, Rachel, had just started working with a different coach, following a different formula. This one was all around setting up a funnel with ads which led to a discovery call and then into an intensive coaching program with a significant investment, much like the one she was signed up for herself.

"My credit cards were already maxed out," Rachel admitted.

"But the coach suggested getting another one. I was feeling pretty desperate, so I thought, 'Hey, what have I got to lose? Things can't get any worse!' So, I went ahead and did it. Plus bought a new designer handbag. The coach said it's important I'm putting across the right image. Fake it til you make it, hey!"

Anna had no idea what to say, "Suppose so!"

Suddenly, Anna was feeling good about her relatively slow and steady growth. She knew that each of these scenarios may work out well for some people, but she couldn't help seeing red flags and financial risk, or at least high pressure. In her own business, she was seeing momentum starting to build and best of all, she had generated this momentum by getting to know her ideal clients and being consistent and responsive. She was creating connections and learning what they responded to and needed. She then focused on creating useful content and offers, which she confidently shared because she knew that her people would more than likely find them helpful. She was starting to realize there was no short cut to getting clear on her own ideal clients and what they wanted and how she could best serve them. It was happening over time, as she continued to experiment and explore what connected for her growing audience and community. Anna had also approached Maha about running a workshop and coaching sessions for each of her staff. Maha had loved the idea and had some great suggestions. As Maha told her what she thought the staff needed, Anna chimed in with ideas about exercises they could do to help the staff feel more empowered and motivated and they created a rough outline for several workshops. After the first they'd have a better idea if some personal coaching might also be helpful. She'd been talking about what she was doing with her hairdresser the other day and her hairdresser expressed interest in running a workshop with her team. She'd jumped on that too and they had a theme and date already sorted. She was feeling really inspired and energised and it felt like that was shining through in every conversation. Opportunities were starting to arise in ways that felt really natural. She had also talked to her HR friends and had some ideas to work on based on their thoughts. More and more, Anna was focusing on her own business and noticing what was working for her and building on that. She knew her progress might be too slow for some of her peers, but right now it was all feeling very stable and grounded. She was enjoying herself and didn't feel stressed or pressured. She didn't feel like she was searching for elusive secrets, systems or for someone else to show her the way. Not anymore. She felt like she was creating a solid foundation.

ALIGN + ATTRACT REFLECTION

Your turn: How are you feeling about your own path and pace of growth? What is currently working well for you and how might you build on that? Is there anything you'd like to change about your current approaches?

FIND THE RIGHT
SUPPORT FOR YOU

*'I am 100% aligned to accessing
the right support for me.'*

Alexa and Anna were at the beach taking a long walk and debriefing about everything that had been going on for them in their lives and businesses lately. Alexa had gone ahead and run her first webinar and sure, she didn't get heaps of people to sign up, but it had actually gone way better than she expected, and she'd happily promoted the recording afterwards. A few of her clients told her they loved it and she'd had several new clients book in after watching it. She sounded really positive. Actually, Alexa had made tons of progress since they last spoke, more than Anna expected. Anna shared a few of the stories she'd heard at the coaching meet up. Lots of positive ones, but also what she'd heard from Rachel and Rahda. She left out names even though

Alexa didn't know these people.

"You know, it's just not what I want," said Alexa. "Stressing myself out by investing so heavily and then needing to get big results to justify it."

"That's what I thought too," agreed Anna. "I mean, I'm happy to learn from others. I've done some good courses. I've had some great coaches. But I'm not in a place right now where I'm looking for big changes or rapid growth and I definitely don't want to learn anyone else's formulas. I'm more or less on track. I just sometimes get in my own way and then have to sort myself out. Sometimes I think more support would be good, but I'm not exactly sure what." Anna and Alexa talked through some of the different options.

"Masterminds always sound so fun," Anna said. "I liked the sound of some of the ones I heard about at that conference I went to."

"Especially the international ones that involve travel and retreats," Alexa agreed.

"Exactly! But I guess we could also just go on a holiday together if that's the main attraction," Anna laughed.

They discussed the idea of creating their own mastermind and then dismissed that. They talked about a few coaches they knew who focused on specific business areas and speculated on the ways working with those could impact on their growth. Anna mentioned a few people she'd met at the conference she went to. They talked about some business courses that might help.

"Honestly, the best support I'm getting for my business right now is from my Kinesiologist," Alexa eventually said.

Anna looked surprised. "But you are a Kinesiologist?"

"Exactly. And I see my own Kinesiologist too. I used to do some swaps with friends, but now I'm paying to see someone who's been in business for years. She's great at what she does, and she gets the business side of things. We focus on that in my sessions and I'm making so much more progress."

Anna had noticed that already. She also noticed that Alexa seemed a lot more confident and sure of herself. That was probably coming across in all areas of her life and contributing to her newfound business success.

"When you say you focus on business stuff with her, what do you mean?" Anna questioned.

She'd had a couple of sessions with Alexa and loved them, but they'd been focused on other things and weren't business related. It hadn't occurred to her to focus on her business.

"Basically, I take everything that is stressing me out about my business into the session. I download all of that. I tell her everything I want to achieve; my income goals, how many clients I want to attract, the impact I want to have, how I want to grow my business. I tell her all my worries and insecurities and how I want to be feeling instead. And you know, she does her thing and out I come, a brand new person." Alexa was laughing.

Anna was aware she was simplifying the process, just a little, but this was really appealing to her. She already knew how personalized Kinesiology sessions were and she could see how doing some more sessions could fit with all the work she was already doing to support her mindset and energy. If she was already doing well, this could take things to a whole new level.

"So, I can take my business goals to her, and she can help me clear my own blocks to achieving those? Oh, my God, that would be so efficient! Wait … do you mind if I go see her and not you?"

"Of course not! I kind of prefer it when my friends work with someone else anyway; it's a better boundary. Plus she works on business stuff, and that's not my thing. I prefer working with health related issues and hormones and emotions. She can have the business stuff!"

Anna was feeling inspired. At this point she didn't want to head off on a completely new tangent or shoot for rapid growth in her business. She wanted help to continue on the track she was already on but to progress a little faster and more smoothly. It was now so important to her that she stay connected to herself and her own path and she had the feeling this was going to really help.

ALIGN + ATTRACT REFLECTION

Your turn: Do you have the support you need right now? If not, what kind of additional support structures do you need? What are your current priorities? As you consider all your options, what do you want to look into further?

CELEBRATE YOUR SUCCESS

'I am 100% aligned to celebrating success.'

Anna had a glass of French champagne in hand, and was sitting opposite Josh. She was in reflection mode. It was one year since she'd left her full-time job. Her year had seen plenty of twists and turns, and she had of course ended up back doing some contract work too, but there was also much to celebrate. She and Josh spoke about some of the wins she'd seen her clients have, the revenue she'd been able to generate from client work, and also from her workshops and corporate speaking. She hadn't even been thinking about workshops or corporate events at the start of the year. It had been a year of new people, experiences and growth, and lots of course-correcting too. They talked about some of the mistakes she'd made early on, and the changes she'd made.

"You're so much more in control now," Josh commented. "You still talk about challenges, but they don't seem to set you back like they did. You seem a lot more confident … about everything really."

Anna was nodding in confirmation. "Yes, that's how I feel. It's like I'm not taking business or myself so seriously anymore. Business feels more like a series of fun challenges and opportunities rather than something I'm hinging all my self-worth on. I know I'm going to keep on learning, making mistakes and changing things and I'm more at peace with that now. I don't feel like I have to rush so much, just keep moving forwards. Make the next decision and take the next action." Josh was nodding. "Before, I felt like I needed things to work in certain ways or it was a reflection on me, but that wasn't right. Now I feel like I can achieve my goals in lots of different ways. I don't even think about other people and their businesses hardly at all anymore either. I used to do that so much! And remember how I used to feel like I had to be working all the time, even if I was just redesigning my logo for the tenth time, or spending a ton of time on social media? Oh, my God, that was crazy!"

Josh cleared his throat, "Yeah, I was glad when that phase passed." They both laughed.

Anna's business endeavours had certainly placed more pressure on their relationship at certain times during the year, but in the last few months they'd settled into a much healthier balance. They were having fun and joking together, and Anna's business was just one of the things they talked about rather than the central topic of discussion every night like it had been for a while.

"I just think I'm getting better at connecting to myself and being clear on what my priorities are. I keep coming back to what

I want, and I keep making decisions and taking actions that are in alignment with what I want. Basically, that's what I've been doing this whole time: I've been creating *alignment*. And, it's working. I'm creating a business and life that I actually love."

ALIGN + ATTRACT REFLECTION

Your turn: What are your biggest takeaways about alignment and how that looks in your own business and life? Did you work through the prompts as you read Anna's story and take time to reflect and take you own action? If you think you can go deeper, go ahead and do that right now. That's how YOU are going to create a business and life that YOU actually love.

I guess there comes time in life where you have to make big decisions and focus on what matters, that's what living in alignment is all about, isn't it?

RESOURCES

TOOLS FOR YOUR ALIGMENT

My vision for *ALIGN + ATTRACT* is more than these pages, below are some resources to help you create the business you're here to create, from a strong energetic centre, your place of integrity.

#Alignandattract

Share your reflections as you read using #alignandattract

Align + Attract

The *Align + Attract* group program contains the techniques I've created + used with hundreds of my entrepreneurial clients to help them release blocks and align to their own goals. We use my unique Alignment Process as our primary tool and dive deep to create energetic alignment in your business (and life). *Align + Attract* helps you connect to your own wisdom, intuition and personal power. If you want to attract more ideal clients and feel solid with your fees and confident as you work towards your next income milestone, this is for you. You can also use my Alignment Process to align your energy to the goals at the start of each chapter in this book. *Align + Attract* is the primary way I work with clients at this time. You can expect personal feedback from me in our wonderfully supportive Facebook group when you join the program, along with live group calls each time a new live round runs, with the archives of all live calls also available as a reference for you: alignandattract.com

DIY Kinesiology Kit

In my *DIY Kinesiology Kit* I teach you how to align your energy to your goals using my Alignment Process. You receive a copy of my *DIY Kinesiology Kit* when you join *Align + Attract*, but this is also a stand-alone product if you want to work independently and don't need all the business alignment resources and additional support that come with *Align + Attract*. You can use it to align to any goal, including those at the start of each chapter of this book: awakenkinesiology.com/courses/diy-kinesiology-kit

Awaken Kinesiology

My *Awaken Kinesiology* website is a hub for all my blog posts, videos and resources. It's also the place where you can find out how you can work with me personally, and find out about new books, programs and free offerings I create: awakenkinesiology. com

Connect with me on social media

Join me at Facebook /awakenkinesiology
and Instagram: /kerryrowett

Journal

The prompts found at the end of each chapter have been collated into a journal for you, which you can download at: alignandattract.com/journal

EFT video

I created an *EFT (Emotional Freedom Technique)* video for you. which you can find at alignandattract.com/eft

Reiki healing

Sign up for a group Reiki healing from me at: awakenkinesiology.com/reiki

ALIGNMENT AFFIRMATIONS

Use these alignment goals as affirmations, or align to each goal using the process I teach in *Align + Attract* or in my *DIY Kinesiology Kit*:

'I'm 100% aligned to being honest with myself.'

'I am 100% aligned to focusing on what I want.'

'I am 100% aligned to being true to myself.'

'I am 100% aligned to being clear on what I want.'

'I am aligned with my business.'

'I am 100% aligned to connecting from my heart.'

'I am aligned with creating a great life as well as a great business.'

'I am aligned to feeling relaxed and clear.'

'I am 100% aligned to trusting myself and life.'

'I am 100% aligned to accepting my best is good enough.'

'I'm 100% clear on who I can help.'

'I am 100% aligned to communicating how I can help.'

'I'm 100% aligned to knowing what is useful
and helpful to my clients.'

'I am aligned to a healthy relationship with my money.'

'I am 100% aligned to healthy boundaries.'

'I am 100% aligned to staying in my own energy.'

'I'm 100% aligned to backing myself.'

'I'm 100% aligned to staying on my own path
and recognising my progress.'

'I am aligned to being inclusive.'

'I'm 100% aligned to staying in my own lane.'

'I am 100% aligned to my own priorities.'

'I am aligned to finding my own solutions
and staying on my own path.'

'I am 100% aligned to accessing the right support for me.'

'I am 100% aligned to celebrating success.'

ABOUT THE AUTHOR

Kerry Rowett is a holistic Kinesiologist who works with her worldwide clientele via Skype and in her group program, *Align + Attract* to help them create powerful changes and alignment in their businesses and lives. She started her business in 2009 and after filling her practice relatively quickly with wonderfully aligned clients, began teaching other practitioners how to align their energy to their business goals in 2011. She believes the answers you seek are inside of yourself, but sometimes you might need support to access these. She also believes life is full of opportunities for growth and in the power of being able to find your way back to your own centre when challenges inevitably occur. Kerry lives in Adelaide, Australia with her beautiful partner Shaun, and gorgeous little boy, Charlie.